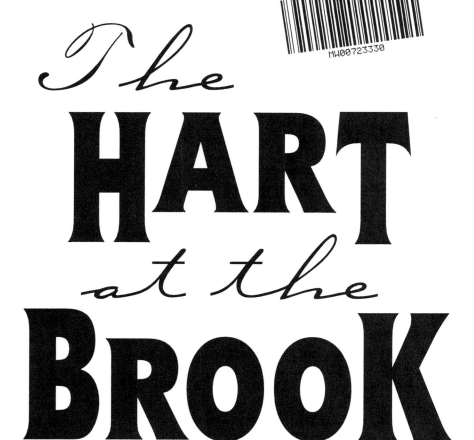

The
HART
at the
BROOK

MW00723330

The HART *at the* BROOK

A Hungering Spirit's Journey to God

Craig Tappe

COLLEGE PRESS
PUBLISHING COMPANY
Joplin, Missouri

Copyright © 1997
College Press Publishing Company

Printed and Bound in the United States of America
All Rights Reserved

All Scripture quotations, unless indicated, are taken from
THE HOLY BIBLE: NEW INTERNATIONAL VERSION®.
Copyright © 1973, 1978, 1984 by International Bible Society.
Used by permission of Zondervan Publishing House.
All rights reserved.

Cover Design by Mark A. Cole

Library of Congress Cataloging-in-Publication Data

Tappe, Craig, 1959–
    The hart at the brook: a hungering spirit's journey to God /
Craig Tappe.
      p.   cm.
    ISBN 0-89900-750-3 (pbk.)
    1. Spiritual life–Christianity. 2. Desire for God. I. Title.
BV4501.2.T26 1997
248.4–dc21
                                         97-11018
                                            CIP

Table of Contents

Introduction

In Psalm 42:1-2 David says, "As the hart pants after the water brooks, so pants my soul after you, O God. My soul thirsts for God, for the living God: When shall I come and appear before God?" (KJV).

Have you ever been thirsty? I do not mean a thirst that can be quenched by a couple of swallows from a water fountain. I am talking about a mouth parching, tongue swelling, throat burning, gut wrenching kind of thirst. You see it on the sidelines during football games. Even in cold weather, the players build up such a thirst that an entire jug of *Gatorade* does not fully satisfy them. As you watch those guys gasping for every swallow they can choke down, you get a fair picture of the kind of thirst David is describing in Psalm 42. But there are two very important differences between David and those football players. First, David's thirst was not felt in his throat, but in the deepest regions of his soul. Second, David's thirst could not be quenched by *Gatorade*. The thirst he is describing is a thirst which can only be satisfied by a close walk with Jehovah God.

A close walk with God — that is what the world is missing today. In fact, many of God's own children are missing out on the fullness that only walking with God can bring them. The very idea for this book was conceived out of a desperate search for God. The search did not begin in my non-Christian days. In fact, I had been preaching for many years when I finally realized how much I was missing in my walk with Jesus. The idea was born in an amazing discovery that God really is personally interested in me. It matured as I learned the daily lesson of what it means to let God have His full control over my life. The journey is not completed yet. In fact, it has just begun. I pray that you will join me as we seek together to quench our growing thirst for God.

Section One

Section 1
Filling The God-Shaped Hole

If you want to get closer to someone in a crowded room, there is only one good way to do it. You have to push through the crowd as you *physically* move your body in the direction of that person. With each step, you move closer and closer.

Our desire for a closer walk with Jesus is not nearly that one dimensional. In fact, before you ever set out to move closer to God, you have to undergo some inward transformation which allows God to move closer to you. There is an old question which asks, "If there is a distance between you and God, who moved?" This question is usually asked in order to point out that the journey back to God is your responsibility. I used to believe that — in the days of my spiritual emptiness. However, I have come to see God as the father in the story of the Prodigal Son. That father did not make his son travel the entire distance. He ran off the porch to meet that boy before he ever made it to the gate. That father made a very aggressive move in order to close the distance between him and his son. You know, God has done the same for us. When we realize how empty we are without Him, He will make some very aggressive efforts to close the gap between us and Him.

In this section we will discuss the emptiness we have within us. We will notice where it comes from, how we get rid of it and what God has done to make fullness possible. It is not a sin to be empty! God's greatest champions have experienced spiritual emptiness. But, emptiness can be deadly if you do not take steps to allow God to fill it.

11

Chapter 1
New Perspectives

The setting was a saloon in "The Old West." As the rough cowboys were sipping on their drinks and filling the air with smoke from their cigars, a small man who was clearly a "city slicker" walked in. He wore nice clothes and shiny shoes as he approached the bar and ordered a drink. One of the cowboys approached him and asked, "You're some kind of furriner, ain't ya?" The man replied, "I guess you could say that. I am from Boston and I am out here prospecting for gold." "Can you dance," asked the cowboy with a sly grin on his face. "No," said the stranger, "but I have always wanted to." "Well I will teach you," said the cowboy as he pulled out his pistol and started shooting at the man's feet. The poor prospector stumbled and stammered all the way out the door. After getting his big laugh, the cowboy went back to his table and finished his drink. When it came time to leave, the cowboy walked out the swinging doors and started to get on his horse. Suddenly, he felt something cold against the back of his head. He turned and found himself looking straight down both barrels of the prospector's 12-gauge shotgun. "Mister, have you ever kissed a horse on the mouth," asked the prospector. "No sir," said the cowboy, "but I have always wanted to."

It is true — you get a little different perspective of things when you look down the barrel of a gun. In Ecclesiastes 3, Solomon mentions something else that gives us a new perspective on life. In verse 11 Solomon says God "set eternity in our hearts." God has placed within the heart of every man a comprehension of something greater than himself. We are left wondering what he is talking about until we get to Ecclesiastes 12. There, Solomon tells us that fearing God and keeping His commandments is "the whole duty of man." If you put these two passages together, you find that this large expanse within our heart is in the shape of God. In other words, only God can fill the deep longing that all of us feel. It does not matter if a person knows why he is empty. It is not important that the person acknowledge God in his life at all. He still feels the emptiness, and he still does what he can to fill it.

Some non-Christians are not even aware of their spiritual need. They feel the emptiness, but many of them do not acknowledge it. Others feel it and acknowledge they are missing something, but they are at a loss to know what to do about it. Some Christians feel the emptiness and even know what to do about it, but are simply too busy with the affairs of their lives to give it a second thought. Still other Christians are aware of the emptiness that sometimes overtakes them, and they want, more than anything in the world, to fill it up. We will focus on these people in this section.

There are Christians who love God very much, but they are continuing to struggle. Some are hung up on a particular area of spiritual growth they just cannot seem to get past. Others are struggling with a sin which has plagued them for years, and they have never been able to overcome it. Still others sit and listen to lessons on the abundance of Christian living and the happiness and joy that comes from walking with Jesus, and they wonder where they missed the boat. You see, these types of Christians love God supremely, and they are thrilled to be children of God, but there is still something missing in their lives. They are snagged on something that will not let them go. God never meant the Christian life to be that way. God means for us to have a daily adventure as we walk with Him. He wants us to experience the fullness of joy, wonder and excitement that only walking with Him can bring us. In spite of all of this, many Christians miss out on large portions of God's plan for their lives. The reason is simple — they are not allowing God to fill up their God-shaped hole. The focus of this chapter will be the person hungering for fullness and the steps he should take to achieve it.

In order to fill our God-shaped hole, we must develop —

1. A Close Communion with God
2. Direction in Life
3. A Dream in Our Hearts

A Close Communion with God

God has always desired us to walk closely with Him. Jesus told the woman at the well that the day was coming when all lovers of God would worship "in spirit and in truth." He went on to say that "God seeks such to worship Him." Did you hear that? God wants us to worship Him. God desires our closeness and our communion. We come to understand this a little better when we hear Him tell us, "I will be a Father to you, and you will be my sons and daughters . . ." (2 Corinthians 6:18). There it is in a nutshell! God sincerely desires us to walk closely with Him for the same reason we desire our children to walk closely with us. He loves us more than even He could ever fully express to us. That is the good news. The bad news is this close communion does not come automatically or magically.

When I was in high school, I played on the tennis team. At the time I was playing, Bjørn Borg was the world champion. I really admired him. In fact, I admired him so much that I tried to be like him. I tried to grow my hair like his, and I wore a head band that looked just like his. I started gripping my racket the way he did, and I even started trying to grow a few whiskers on my chin. I did anything I could to be just like Bjørn Borg. But you know what? When I got on the tennis court, I did not play like Bjørn Borg at all. That confused me a little bit. How could I do all these outward things just like he did and still not play like he played? The answer is obvious, isn't it? I forgot there was more to Bjørn Borg's tennis than I could see. While I imitated those things which I saw him do, there was a whole world of things that I never saw him do. For instance, I never saw him get up at the crack of dawn and exercise. I never saw the countless hours of just serving balls across the net. I never saw all of the hidden things that Bjørn did that made him the greatest tennis player who ever lived. You see, it takes more than a headband to play tennis like Bjørn Borg. It takes a lifetime of grueling practice and exercise.

When I look at God's champions in the Scriptures, I am really impressed. I look at Moses as he led God's people out of Egypt, and I sit in wonder at his bravery and commitment to God. I look at Elijah as he boldly preached God's message to a group of people who really did not want to hear it, and I wish I could have that kind of determination. I see Jesus in all of His wisdom and compassion, and I long to be like Him. But you know, no matter how much I try to imitate their outward actions, I will never be the champions they were until I examine their unseen lives. In Exodus 3 Moses spent forty years in the wilderness of Midian. While there tending sheep, he likely spent many hours alone with God. In 1 Kings 19 we see Elijah's experience with God in the desert. While there, God spoke to him and told him what he needed to do to be revived in his service to God. Jesus spent forty days in the wilderness fasting and praying to His Father (Luke 4). This was the secret of all three of these men. Each of them was a champion for God because each of them spent a great deal of time alone with God. Time to pray, to meditate, to focus with a clear mind on what God is trying to tell you — these are the things which will give you a close communion with Jesus.

So many Christians ignore the truth of this principle. They are too busy with their own routines. They wake up each morning, and they get ready for work. They go to work, and they come home. When they get home, they eat, take their shower, and watch TV for awhile before they go to bed. When they wake up, they start the same merry-go-round all over again. On the weekends, they busy themselves with sports, Scouts, and other activities with their families. By the time they get to the end of the week, they realize they have spent little, if any, time alone with God. Is it a mystery that these people have limited communion with God? Is it any secret that their God-shaped hole remains unfilled, and they find themselves growing weaker in their faith and their devotion to God? They have simply not invested themselves in the activities that produce a close walk with God. The first step toward filling the God-shaped hole is developing a close communion with God.

Direction in Life

God strongly desires us to have a meaningful direction in our lives. That is not surprising since we have already seen how much God loves us. But, He does not simply inform us that we should have direction. He teaches us the kind of direction we should have. As we will see, not just any direction will lead us to fullness. In fact, only one direction will do that. Paul expresses it well in 1 Corinthians 10:31 where he tells us to "do it all for the glory of God." In Philippians 1:21 he says, "For to me, to live is Christ and to die is gain." You see, whether Paul was alive or dead, his goal was to serve and to walk with Christ. We see a graphic picture of what Paul is describing in Matthew 14. Peter and the other apostles were in a ship in the middle of a storm on the Sea of Galilee. As they were struggling to avoid disaster, they saw a figure of a man walking across the water. Thinking it was a ghost, they cried out in fear. Jesus comforted them by identifying Himself. Peter was the first to speak, "Lord, if it really is you, tell me to walk out on the water to you." Jesus told him to come on out of the boat. Peter stepped out of the boat and walked several steps toward Jesus. That is God's desire for us. He wants us to have Him as our direction. He wants us to "step out of the boat" and allow Him to guide every step of our way.

Sometimes we have a difficult time buying into all of that. We go through life trying to be the very best employees we can be. We read and listen to talk shows in an effort to be the best parents we can be. Christian athletes, teachers, and business people all want to excel in their fields. In order to succeed in these areas, we go about it in the same way the world does — under our own power. We work ourselves to death in an effort to grab that "brass ring." All the while we are doing this, we experience only limited success in these areas. We find that our lives are a constant struggle as we work to get ahead, and our God-shaped hole just empties more and more. The problem is our direction. You cannot set out to be the very best in a dozen different areas and expect to succeed. You need a single focus. That is why God tells us to seek His kingdom first. You see, if you seek to walk closely with God in every area of your life, you will automatically excel in the rest of these areas. The best parent in the world will be the person who walks most closely to God. The most efficient employee and the most successful teacher will be the person who loves God and seeks to please Him in all he does. It is only logical. If I am working to please myself or some other man, I am only going to go so far and then I will stop. On the other hand, if I am intending to please God in all I do, I will work tirelessly until I accomplish that. If you want to fill your God-shaped hole, you have to develop a God-centered direction in your life.

A Dream in Your Heart

Did you know that many of God's champions were dreamers? What I mean is, they had a vision of something they wanted to accomplish for God, and they worked tirelessly to see it become a reality. For example, David was a man after God's own heart. Part of the reason for that was he loved God enough to want to do something great for Him. In 2 Samuel 7 we read where David got the idea to build a house for God. While David himself was not able to build it, he set things in motion so that his son, Solomon, could complete the job. Nehemiah had a dream of returning to Jerusalem which had lain in ruins for years since the forces of Babylon came through town. The book of Nehemiah shows how God was able to make that dream come true. Dreaming has not gone out of style today. God still expects His people to be dreamers. Ephesians 3:20 tells us that God is able to make our wildest dreams come true. Whatever you want to accomplish for God is at your fingertips. Judging from some of the science fiction movies that have been made, humans are quite capable of dreaming up some pretty wild things. But God assures us that we cannot out-dream Him. Whatever we can conceive in our heart to do for God, He can do through us!

Before you get going too fast on that thought, you need to beware of a "bridge out ahead." It is true that God is able to do amazing things through His children. However, the tragedy is that very few of His children dream anymore. Think about yourself for a moment. When is the last time you had a bold dream for God? When it comes to the present, most of us think in terms of our own limitations. These limitations come in the form of physical abilities, talents, time, money and a variety of other things. The bottom line is this — we make our plans in view of how far these things will take us and then we quit. There is no room for dreaming in that way of thinking. When it comes to the future, we probably think very little about it at all. When suggestions are made regarding the work of your church, how many times has someone suggested that the matter be tabled until the next meeting so we can give some thought and prayer to it? When the next meeting comes around, how many times has it become painfully obvious that no one has even given a second thought to the matter, much less prayed about it? You see, we talk a much better game than we play.

The result of this pitiful approach to life is we take life as it comes. We give no thought to what God is able to do through us. Consequently, we are limited by what we are able to see and touch. As we live life in this way, our God-shaped hole remains unfilled and we miss out on the thrill of seeing God bring our dreams to life. In order for our God-shaped hole to begin filling up, we must develop the practice of dreaming wild dreams for God. With Him working in us, we will see each of them come true, one at a time.

Conclusion

In order to fill our God-shaped hole we must have a new perspective. We must realize that we have a hole in our hearts and only God can fill it. That hole begins filling up as we develop a close, daily communion with Him. It continues to fill up as we make Him the direction of our lives. It reaches the brim when we begin dreaming dreams for Him and allowing Him to make them come true.

Harriet Beecher Stowe won many literary honors in her lifetime. Her first public recognition came when she was only 12 years old. Her father was a professor at a university at the time. In an assembly where the entire student body and faculty were present, one of her essays was read. She was in the audience, and her father was seated on the stage. When the reading was completed, the entire audience gave a lengthy standing ovation. When the author's identity was revealed, Harriet's father was beaming with pride. She later stated that no honor ever given her in her life was as special as the smile on her father's face on that occasion.

As we walk with God, it should be our highest goal to make our Father proud of us. It should give us great joy and fullness to know we have brought a smile across His beautiful face by the lives we are living. This is possible only if we have a relationship with Him. When that becomes the overruling purpose of our lives, our God-shaped hole will begin filling up, and we will be on our way to never being the same again.

Discussion Questions

1. Why do many people seek to ignore the emptiness inside?

2. Why do many people refuse to turn to God for filling?

3. What specific things cause your God-shaped hole to become empty in your life?

4. When is the best time of day for you to spend in communion with God?

5. In what ways do you feel your communion with God is lacking?

6. How does being a Christian cause you to be the best in whatever role you may choose for your life?

7. Why do so many Christians experience only limited success in their various fields?

8. What is God's desire for us regarding our dreams?

9. What specific dreams do you have for your service to God?

10. What specific dreams do you have for your congregation in the next five years?

Chapter 2
New Understanding

Most of the problems people experience in marriage stem from unfulfilled expectations. No matter how long two people have known each other, there is something about living in the same house that brings out all of the things we never knew before about the other person. I recently ran across an article which explains this very well. It is divided into two sections. The first section is entitled, "What Every Man Expects." Under that category it says — "She will always be beautiful and cheerful. She will have hair that never needs curlers or beauty shops. She will never be sick — just allergic to jewelry and fur coats. She will insist that moving the furniture by herself is good for her figure. She will be an expert in cooking, cleaning house, fixing the car or TV, painting the house and being quiet. Her favorite hobbies will be mowing the lawn and shoveling snow. She will hate charge cards."

The second section is entitled, "What He Gets." Notice some of the things in this section — "She speaks 140 words per minute with gusts up to 180. She was once a model for a totem pole. Where there's smoke, there she is — cooking. She lets you know you have only two faults — everything you say and everything you do. No matter what she does with her hair, it looks like an explosion at a steel wool factory. If you get lost, open your wallet and she will find you."

While this article is really silly, it points out the difference between what we expect and what we get many times. We often do not even live up to our own expectations. We certainly do not always live up to God's expectations of us. Disappointing ourselves and our Father has a gradual emptying effect on us. Throughout the book of Ephesians we are told of a variety of ways in which God wants to fill us up.

In Ephesians 1, we are immediately told that God wants to fill us up. In verse 3 He says He has given us "every spiritual blessing." In verse 23 Jesus is referred to as, "the fullness of him who fills everything in every way." God recognizes our need for Him in order to have fullness in our lives. In verses 15-23 Paul explains that this filling up process begins when we understand some things about our relationship with God. That is why he says he was praying for the Ephesians that "the eyes of your heart may be enlightened" (verse 18). As we go through this point, the real tragedy of emptiness will come to light: there is no reason for it. God has provided everything we need to be full and happy. Many are missing out on these things because they are ignorant of the basic elements of their relationship with their Father. What are some of these elements? Hope, acceptance, and power.

Hope

In Ephesians 1:18 Paul identifies the first thing to which he wants our eyes to be opened. He wants us to know "the hope to which he has called you." Now, what exactly do we need to understand about our hope? First, we need to understand it is a hope of salvation. We must realize we have been saved from death in Hell for all eternity. We also need to understand that salvation is not hard to get. Romans 10:6-9 uses some obscure language, but the basic meaning is that the salvation God offers is very accessible to all. In Romans 5:8 Paul adds to that by saying, "While we were still sinners, Christ died for us." Do you get the picture? We were totally helpless and hopeless. There was nothing we could do to solve our sin problem. Some may object by saying, "I had to believe" or "I had to be baptized." These actions of obedience did not earn you anything. Even after you did these things, God still did not have to save you. God granted us salvation *in spite* of what we have done and not *because* of it. He lets us keep it for the same reason.

There are many ways someone can misunderstand the hope God has given us. Some have the false notion that once we have salvation, there is nothing we can do to lose it. Others think this kind of hope encourages people to continue to sin without a second thought about it. Both of these notions are a misunderstanding of hope. The proper understanding will liberate us from the thought that we must measure up to a certain standard before we can be acceptable to God. As a result, we will overflow in our love and gratitude toward God. Because of that love and gratitude, we will determine to serve and to please God in all we do. During this entire process we will find our God-shaped hole beginning to fill up.

Acceptance

Paul also tells us our eyes should be open to "the glory of His inheritance in the saints." If you read very casually, you may think he is still discussing our inheritance in Heaven. But look again. This phrase is talking about "His inheritance." Did you know God has an inheritance just like we do? Our inheritance is Heaven. But God already has Heaven. What God longs for is *us*. Can you imagine that? Think of all the bad things you have done. In spite of it all, God wants you. We are not talking about a casual acceptance where God nonchalantly shrugs His shoulders and accepts you. We are talking about the ecstatic joy of a shepherd who finds a lost sheep. We are talking about the gladness of a woman who finds a very valuable coin she has misplaced. We are talking about the unspeakable delight of a father who runs off the porch and down the road to greet a returning son. This is the kind of overflowing acceptance God gives us. To top it off, we did nothing to earn God's acceptance. God accepts us (warts and all) just because He loves us. You do not find that kind of acceptance anywhere in this world. People everywhere are looking for it, but no human being is able to give it.

In Hebrews 10, God makes a deal with us. In verse 17 He says He will forget about all our sins. That is the total acceptance for which people throughout the world are searching. In return, God wants us to "draw near" to Him (verse 22). That is what we are talking about throughout this book — drawing near to God and allowing Him to draw near to us. When we understand the acceptance God has given us, our God-shaped hole will get fuller and fuller.

Power

In verses 19-22 of Ephesians, chapter 1, Paul tells us about the power God displayed in the life of Jesus Christ. God not only raised Him from the dead, but He set Him up as King over "all authority and power," and made him the head of the body, which is the church.

The same power is available today to those who believe. God is able to do some amazing things in the life of someone who is willing to be used by Him. For instance, through God's power we can resist temptation and defeat Satan. 1 Peter 5:8-9 describes Satan as "a roaring lion." Have you ever been to the zoo? Most of the time the lions are lazily laying in the sun. The reason they are so calm is they are full. The zookeeper keeps them well fed, so they have no reason to get up and roam around. But you see a different picture at feeding time when the lions are hungry. A hungry lion paces back and forth and roars loudly to signal he is ready to eat. That is how Peter describes Satan. But there is no reason to be frightened of him. As long as we draw near to God, we can resist Satan and he will run away from us (James 4:7).

In addition to our battle with Satan, we also need God's help in our battle with ourselves. In Galatians 5 we are told of many qualities of character God wants us to have. A casual glance over this list will cause the average Christian to realize how far away he is from being what God wants him to be. But there is hope! God is there to help us with these things. That is why these qualities are called "the fruit of the Spirit." It is God's Spirit working within us that makes it possible for us to grow in these ways.

So he would not leave anything out, Paul brings all of this to a conclusion in Philippians 4:13 where he says, "I can do *everything* through him who gives me strength" (emphasis added). Whether you are talking about your battle with Satan, yourself or any other challenge, God's power is there to help you succeed. We do not have to face anything in this life alone. God's power is at our disposal any hour of the day or night. When that really sinks into our hearts, we will begin enjoying some of the fullness God has in mind for His children.

Conclusion

Many faithful Christians are missing out on huge portions of God's plan for them. Many go through life without experiencing the abundance and joy God wants to give them. Many are struggling with a sin that just keeps returning to them. Consequently, their spiritual growth has slowed to a crawl, and they are not enjoying a deep, meaningful relationship with God. The tragedy is it does not have to be that way. God has given us hope, acceptance, power and everything else we need. All we have to do is understand these things and we will be well on the way to fullness.

Timothy Richards was a missionary to China for the latter part of his life. He was visiting with a Chinese businessman on one occasion when the man informed Richards that he had read the New Testament through three times. Richards asked him what he thought about the Bible. The man responded, "The most marvelous thing that impressed me was the thought that it is possible for men to become temples of the Holy Spirit." You know, this still has not dawned on many of God's children. They go through life feeling afraid, alone, and quite empty. They know God is only an arm's length away, but they are so tied up with their schedules and activities, they just seem to crowd Him out of their lives. What a tragic existence this is for people who were meant to be filled up with Jesus! When we allow Jesus to fill us up, we will enjoy a life that we never dreamed possible before!

Discussion Questions

1. In what ways do we disappoint ourselves?

2. What kinds of things does God give us to fill us up?

3. How does biblical hope affect you?

4. Why do humans crave acceptance so much?

5. How does God's acceptance of us differ from the world's acceptance?

6. What kind of power does God offer us today?

7. In what specific ways do you need God to transform your life?

Chapter 3
New Choices

Song leaders sometimes try to get creative as they lead the congregation in worship. There was one song leader who chose to mix it up on one song. He said, "I want the women to sing the verse 'I will go home today' and I want the men to come in on the chorus, ' Glad day, Glad day.'"

Making wrong choices can sometimes be funny and mildly embarrassing. There are other times when wrong choices are much more serious. Many faithful Christians struggle with emptiness and God wants us to turn to Him for fullness. In Ephesians 1 we saw that fullness comes from having a proper understanding. In Chapter 2 we are told that fullness comes from making the right choices.

The problem began when we sinned (verses 1-3). At that point, we were emptied by death and rebellion. God's mercy entered the picture and saved us from all of that (verses 4-9). Consequently, we have become "dwellings in which God lives" (verse 22). That simply means God is inside us, filling us up. Some of God's people have escaped the death and rebellion of sin, but they are still running on empty. The reason is because of the choices they are making.

A Contrast of Conditions

Ephesians 2 begins by discussing the condition of spiritual emptiness. In that condition, we *lived for our own desires* (verse 3). God makes it clear in many places that you cannot be successful in life by doing things your own way. You may think you are going the right way, but the final destination is death (Proverbs 14:12). As a result, any who guide their own way end up wandering aimlessly and wasting their lives (Ecclesiastes 1:14). This explains why so many people are living in despair and depression. Homes are broken, people resort to drugs and alcohol to solve their problems, teenagers are strapped with unwanted pregnancies, and all of it is because they are trying to fill themselves up.

In the days of our spiritual emptiness we lived *outside of God's family* (verse 12). Do you remember how miserable the Prodigal Son was until he decided to go back home? That is the kind of emptiness we experience without God in our lives. Verse 12 also shows that we were *outside of God's promises.* As great as Moses was, he did something which displeased God greatly. As a result, God would not allow him to enter the promised land of Canaan. There were a few times that Moses asked God to reconsider, but God was determined. In Deuteronomy 3:24-27 we read the final conversation that God and Moses had on the subject. God told Moses to drop it because He was not going to change His mind. However, God allowed Moses to get on top of Mount Pisgah, which was just on the edge of the Jordan River. From the summit of Pisgah, Moses could see the promised land, but he could not enter it. What longing and regret Moses must have felt as he gazed upon that marvelous sight. This is the kind of feeling we have when we are empty today. We see the abundance and joy that others experience, and we wonder how we can get it.

Finally, verse 12 says we had *no access to God.* That was what the rich man experienced when he looked up to find himself in torment while Lazarus was safe in the bosom of Abraham. When he requested that Lazarus be sent with some water, the rich man was told there was a "great chasm" between where he was and where Lazarus was. That simply means he had absolutely no way to get to God. Can you imagine how desperate and alone he must have felt? Can you imagine how it would feel not to be able to talk to God? It would be like being trapped on the top floor of a building while it was on fire. You can cry and you can scream to the top of your lungs, but no one can hear you. That is the condition of spiritual emptiness.

Next, Paul turns his attention to the condition of spiritual fullness. Verse 10 tells us that we were created to serve God. Instead of living to fulfill our own desires, we *live to fulfill God's desires for us.* As we mentioned earlier, that will make us the best parent, the best employee, the best mate, or the best of whatever we try to be.

In addition, it will fill us up with joy, peace, assurance, and countless other things for which the world is searching.

Verse 13 says we are *partakers of God's promises*. Paul says, "you who were once far away have been brought near through the blood of Christ." Now, what does that have to do with being a partaker of God's promises? Hebrews 7:19 says, "The law made nothing perfect, but the bringing in of a better hope did; by which we draw near to God" (KJV, adapted). The "better hope" is the new covenant (promise) God made with us. What was the result of this promise? We can "draw near to God." So, when we return to Ephesians 2:13 we see that "drawing nearer" to God is possible only because of God's promises.

No longer do we have to stand on the outside and look in. The days are past when we looked with envy at the abundance others were enjoying. No more do we have to stand on the mountain longingly wishing we could be a part of God's promises. We are part of God's promises and our God-shaped hole can now begin filling up.

Verse 18 says we have *access to God*. In the Old Testament, it was very difficult to have direct access to God. If you wanted to approach God, you had to go through a priest who would take your sacrifices into the Temple and offer them for you. 1 Peter 2:5 says we are now "a holy priesthood" and we can offer our own sacrifices to God. In other words, because of Jesus, we have our own "hot line to God." We no longer have to sit on the other side of a "great gulf" hopelessly crying to have a relationship with God. We can call upon our Father at any time and know He is there.

Finally, verses 19-21 say *we are part of God's family*. He calls us "fellow citizens with God's people and members of God's household." 1 Timothy 3:14-15 also refers to us as "God's household." When the New Testament mentions someone's house, it is usually talking about his family. Therefore, when Paul says we are "the household of God," he is saying we are God's family. What a refreshing change that is from sitting in a pigpen wishing we could be with our Father! Because of Jesus, we are back home again. Because of Jesus, we are a part of God's wonderful family.

Now that we have seen the contrast of emptiness and fullness, we are in a position to see that both of these conditions are a matter of personal choice. Emptiness causes us to live after our own purposes while fullness causes us to seek out God's purposes. Emptiness keeps us outside God's family while fullness puts us into God's family. Emptiness puts us outside God's promises, and fullness allows us to partake of God's promises. Finally, emptiness eliminates all access to God while fullness gives us daily access to God.

In the face of these facts, many Christians continue to make the choices of emptiness. For instance, some of God's children continue to live after their own purposes. They establish their own priorities and manage their own affairs to the extent that there is little room for God's plan in their lives. Some choose not to draw near to God. It is not a concious choice, but they are so busy with their jobs, their families and other activities that they have little time for study, prayer, meditation and communion with God. Many Christians refuse to exercise their access to God. They have a difficult time accepting God's grace, so they busy themselves trying to earn their own salvation. They set up certain standards for themselves. When they fail to measure up, the guilt begins stacking up and they never experience the freedom of God's wonderful forgiveness. Finally, many Christians make a conscious choice not to draw near to God's family. They may worship regularly, and they may fellowship once a month, but they refuse to establish real friendships and real kinship with their brethren. When it comes to being vitally involved in the lives of their fellow-Christians, they do not even know where to begin.

Any one of these choices of emptiness can cause your God-shaped hole to run on empty. If you make two or more of these choices on a regular basis, it could possibly kill you spiritually. Our challenge is to make the choices of fullness every day of our lives so that our thirst for God can be quenched.

Discussion Questions

1. What kinds of choices make you empty in your life?

2. Why do we live for our own desires instead of consulting God's will?

3. When are we most likely to follow our own way and ignore God's way?

4. What does it mean to be outside of God's family?

5. What specific effects does it have to be outside God's promises?

6. Describe what it means to be spiritually full.

7. What does drawing nearer to God have to do with being partakers of God's promises?

8. Why is spiritual fullness better than emptiness?

9. In view of these things, why do some continue to make the choices of emptiness?

Chapter 4

New Priorities

He was an old farmer who had never spent money foolishly. In fact, some would even say he was a little tight where money was concerned. When the fair came to town, he decided that he and his wife would go. While there, they noticed a man who was giving airplane rides for $10 apiece. That was too much for the old farmer to pay, so the pilot offered a deal. He said if the farmer and his wife could go through the entire plane ride without uttering a sound, he would not charge them anything. A free ride sounded great to the old man, so he and his wife got in the back seat of the plane. The pilot took off and began to do daring acrobatic tricks in an effort to get the two people to say something, but neither of them did. The plane did nose dives and turned over upside down several times, but, still, there was no sound from the couple. Finally, the pilot landed the plane and said to the farmer, "If I had not been there, I would never have believed it. You two never uttered a sound." The farmer replied, "It wasn't easy either. I almost said something when my wife fell out." That old farmer clearly had a confused set of priorities.

The same thing becomes apparent when we look into our spiritual lives. People put last things first, and never have time to consider the first things. So, they continue struggling with emptiness. Many begin to get empty when they hit a snag in their spiritual growth. They may be growing in some areas, but there are other areas in which they never seem to grow. As a result, they find themselves looking and acting very much like the world around them. Many times, they postpone their responsibilities before God and tend to their own affairs of life. They have the ability to get very enthused over unimportant things (e.g., sports, hunting, crafts, shopping), but things related to God's service bore them to death. Sometimes people become addicted to something. Addictions of any type have a real emptying impact. Some are addicted to cigarettes. Others are addicted to food. Still others are addicted to work. The list of addictions could go on and on. The point is, being addicted means you have to have something. There is an unbearable emptiness within until the addiction is satisfied. Regardless of its object, the addiction itself empties us for one simple reason. If we are hungrily seeking out our addiction, we are not seeking out God. You see, *He* wants to be our addiction. God wants us to hungrily search after Him. If we give that kind of devotion to something else, our God-shaped hole becomes quite empty.

God recognizes our tendency toward spiritual emptiness. Every chapter in Ephesians mentions a way in which God wants to fill us up. When we get to chapter 3, Paul is discussing some down time the Ephesians were having because of his suffering (verse 13). The remainder of the chapter tells us how to make use of our down times. There is a place of business in my home town which has a sign posted for all employees to see. It says, "Down time is cleaning time." In other words, when their employees have nothing to do, they are expected to clean the area around them. As I read that sign, I thought how appropriate that is for Christians today. God puts a sign for all to see which says, "Down time is leaning time." God understands our down times. God understands when we get discouraged, lonely, tired, or depressed. He wants so badly to fill us up during those times. In Ephesians 3:14-19 God mentions two things which will fill us up during our down times.

Stability of Faith

Verses 14-17 show us that fullness comes from being "rooted and grounded" in our faith. In Colossians 2:7 Paul uses two different terms to make this point. First, he says we should be "rooted." That is an agricultural term which refers to the root system of a tree. It is in the Greek past tense which refers to something that was done at one time in the past, and is not being repeated in the present. He also says we should be "built up." This is an architectural term which refers to the construction of a building. This term is in the Greek present tense which refers to something which was begun in the past and will continue to be done in the present. So, the stability God wants us to have has a definite beginning point (i.e. when we became His children). It is also a growing process which we experience every day of our lives as long as we are walking with Jesus.

Occasionally our lives are absolutely turned upside down. At times it seems that life is crashing in all around us and we feel like we are being uprooted. At those times, we experience a deep sense of emptiness inside. We need to return to the center (stability) and allow God to fill us up again.

David struggled with sin. The result of his sin with Bathsheba is recorded for us in Psalm 51. It is there that he pours his heart of agony and emptiness out to God. Out of that agony, he talks about the bones that God had broken within him. He begs God to return the joy of his salvation to him and not to remove the Holy Spirit from him. David was as dry as a bone spiritually, and it was all because of sin. Christians get caught up in sin. As we noted earlier, sometimes it is a sin which enslaves them for many years. The Bible refers to those as "besetting sins." Other Christians struggle with sin on an impulsive, occasional basis. In either case, sin is an extremely emptying experience. In this situation, we need to repent of our sin from a broken heart and return to God so He can fill us up again.

Job suffered from emptiness for an altogether different reason. Job experienced the loss of his family, his health, and his livelihood in a very brief moment of time. When you read Job's description of himself in Job 30:27-31, it becomes apparent he was suffering from a bad case of emptiness due to the losses he experienced.

Christians are emptied by similar experiences. Many lose their jobs, their loved ones, and their dignity all in one fatal blow. Many go on to lose their peace, their knowledge of what to do next and, sometimes, even their will to go on. As these feelings begin to grow and the God-shaped hole gets more and more empty, many of these people become sluggish in their attendance, lukewarm in their worship and inactive in other areas of service. In short, they do all the wrong things, and they just keep getting more and more barren in their souls. These people need to rearrange their priorities and reorganize their lives so that communion with God is their primary concern. Loss is not an easy thing to experience, but cutting off the fellowship with God and going it by yourself does not make it any easier.

Elijah experienced emptiness when he fought a bout with discouragement. He had just won a tremendous victory over the prophets of Baal in 1 Kings 18. Queen Jezebel did not appreciate it, so she sent him a threatening letter in chapter 19. Out of fear and discouragement, Elijah left town and went into the desert. He sat under a tree and prayed for God to take his life. Have you ever been that empty before? I have known many who have been. The reason for Elijah's emptiness was deep down discouragement!

The story is told of Satan deciding to go out of business. He was selling all of his tools such as greed, lust, hatred, and deceit. The highest priced tool was a well-worn and wedge-shaped instrument. When he was asked about the little device, he explained that it was one of his favorite tools. He claimed that it worked when all the other tools failed. Like a wedge driven by a hammer, this little instrument can be driven deeply into the human soul. Its name was discouragement. There is much truth in that story. Humans become discouraged for a wide variety of reasons. Some experience problems at work or at home, and they become discouraged. Others feel their work in the church is not accomplishing anything or that they are not appreciated. All of these things can bring discouragement into the heart of a child of God.

John the Baptist suffered from emptiness in Luke 7:19 when he was locked up in prison, awaiting his execution. He had preached about Jesus, and he had played his role in God's scheme of redemption in a marvelous way. Now he was coming to the end, and he was beginning to wonder if he had wasted his life. He sent some of his friends to ask Jesus if He were the Messiah or not. I know exactly how John felt. I have experienced doubt which has led to some serious emptiness inside. Sometimes we doubt ourselves and the direction we have chosen for our lives. Sometimes we doubt Jesus in the sense that we are not sure we want Him to be the ruler of our lives. At other times we doubt whether the things we do in our service to God really make any difference at all. When these doubts arise and the emptiness comes, we need reassurance and confirmation.

These are many of the emptying experiences which turn our lives upside down. In order for our emptiness to be filled, we must return to the center of our faith, look to God for our strength and enjoy the ride.

An Awareness of Love

Verses 17-19 show that fullness comes from being aware of how much God loves you. The love of God is so awesome that Paul says it "surpasses knowledge." There was once a soldier who got into some trouble overseas. He turned his back on God and on everything he knew was right. The thing which kept him from falling completely away was the memory of a mother who was back home praying for him. He remembered his entire family and how much they loved him. You know, love is a powerful thing. When life comes tumbling in on us and we find ourselves getting increasingly empty, it helps to know our Father loves us. John wrote to people who were in a great deal of trouble and he said, "To him who loves us and has freed us from our sins by his blood" (Revelation 1:5). The Hebrew writer wrote to people who were in the depths of doubt and he said, "Let us fix our eyes on Jesus . . . who for the joy set before him endured the cross, scorning the shame . . ." (Hebrews 12:2-4). If you are being emptied in your life and are feeling alone and afraid, just remember that God loves you and He is going to take care of you!

It is true — sometimes life throws us a curve ball and we are left feeling extremely empty. Because of this emptiness, we get snagged on some area of our spiritual development. Feelings of being an outsider cause apathy to set in, and we begin to procrastinate the really important thing in our lives. That is the time when we really need to be filled up again.

During World War II, a preacher was called to the home of a father who had just received word of the death of his only son. The father was pacing the floor in grief and asking, "Where was God when my son was being killed?" After a lengthy silence, the preacher responded, "I guess where he was when *His* Son was being killed." Get the picture and remember it — God loves you! God cares for you! God wants you to be filled up with Him even in the down times of your life!

Discussion Questions

1. What are some specific causes for emptiness?

2. What produces "down times" in our lives?

3. What things does God do for us in our down times?

4. What specific things must we have in order to prevent emptiness in our down times?

5. What do we need in order to stabilize our faith in times of struggling with sin?

6. What do we need in order to stabilize our faith in times of loss?

7. What do we need in order to stabilize our faith in times of discouragement?

8. What do we need in order to stabilize our faith in times of doubt?

9. How does love help us to get through our down times?

Chapter 5
New Maturity

Growing up can be quite an experience. One guy was talking about his childhood and how difficult it was to learn how to swim. "My dad took me out to the middle of the lake and threw me in the water. The swim back was not too bad — it was getting out of that gunnysack." Neil Sedaka had a hit song in the 70's called "Breaking Up Is Hard To Do." Someone should rewrite that song to say, "Growing Up Is Hard To Do," because it certainly is. It is not only true physically, but it is also difficult to grow up spiritually.

In Ephesians 4:11-13 Paul discusses this very process. He tells us how God placed people within the church with certain gifts. These gifts were given to assist in building up the body of Jesus. In verse 13 Paul mentions God's desire for us to "become mature, attaining to the whole measure of the fullness of Christ." There it is! Paul is talking about the fullness we have been noticing throughout the book of Ephesians. But this time the fullness in 4:13 is linked to "becoming mature." So, there is a direct link between *filling up with* Jesus and *growing up in* Jesus. You cannot have much of one without the other. In Ephesians 4:14-16 Paul spells out some of the things which are necessary in order for us to grow up in the Lord. Growing up in Jesus involves —

Refusing To Buy into Lies

Growing up in the Lord involves refusing to be thrown off course by different types of false teaching (verse 14). In Paul's world there were two dominant lies which did a great deal of damage to the first century church. One such teaching was called "antinomianism." This was the belief that God's grace would cover everything, no matter what. Open rebellion against God's will was a characteristic of people who held to this belief. "Gnosticism" was another teaching that confused many of the first century Christians. This teaching stated there are two basic elements in the world — flesh and spirit. Flesh is totally evil and spirit is totally good. Consequently, spirit and flesh could have no direct contact with one another. In other words, man could not have any direct contact with God. Paul was telling the Ephesians that growing up in the Lord (filling up) involves refusing to accept these lies.

It is dangerous to believe these lies died in the first century. They are still alive and well among us today. They come in different forms, and they are called by different names, but they are still essentially the same. Antinomianism is still alive in those who have certain nagging problems and have given up on trying to overcome them. Some experience that with sin. They just keep doing the same things week after week and have quit trying to do anything about it. Others have priority problems. They do not attend, give, visit, or teach anyone about Jesus. Sometimes they will even joke and laugh about their confused priorities, but they never do anything to change. Some Christians have attitude problems. They have held resentment toward someone for years and have given up trying to overcome it. They hold on to hard feelings toward parents, children, a boss, a mate or a friend. The facts and the people involved vary from person to person, but the basic problem remains the same — deep down resentment and grudge-bearing. It is vital to be clear on this point. The problem with these folks is *not* that they have these difficulties. The problem is they have given up on trying to overcome them. If that were not bad enough, they also feel that all is well between them and God. They rest in a false assurance that God understands their rebellion and accepts them anyway. This was a lie in Paul's day, and it still is.

Gnosticism is also still making its round among God's people. A more modern name for it might be "the bootstrap mentality." Many Christians know that God is with them, and they even believe He is cheering them on in their lives. However, they approach life like they are on their own. There used to be a very popular song entitled "From A Distance." It has a beautiful tune, but some of the words are rather disturbing. At one point in the song, it says, "God is watching us, God is watching us, God is watching us . . . from a distance." While this may sound very religious and inspiring, it is

Gnosticism to the core. It basically says that we are on our own, and we have to do the best we can for ourselves. This way of thinking fits right in to the way most Americans were raised. You have heard of the "self-made man." That is a person who started from nothing and worked his way up to realize "The American Dream." These kinds of people tend to be quite proud of themselves and equally intolerant of others who have not attained their same level of achievement. These people are easy to spot by the way they talk. They talk a great deal about luck and very little about God's providence. Typically, they have no concept of how God and His will fits into their lives at all. They also talk a great deal about their hard work and the things they have done, but they talk very little (if at all) about what God has done through them. When they talk about the future, it is always in terms of what they can do and what opportunities they will have. They never mention what God would like them to do or what God's plans for the future may be.

Now, when you ask these people, "What about God? Didn't He have anything to do with your success," they are quick to defend themselves by saying, "Well, that's what I meant." But you know what? That is not what they said. Jesus told us whatever is on our heart has a way of coming out in our words. If you can talk a blue streak about your life and your accomplishments without mentioning God's influence a single time, it is probably because you really do not feel He had a great deal to do with it. God is not an afterthought — He is our power. God is not an underlying cause of things that happen — He is leading in front of the pack!

The two lies that threw many first century Christians off track are still very much alive and among us today. Growing up in the Lord and filling up with Jesus begins when you realize you are not alone. When you discover you are walking on top of God's feet with every step you take, life becomes a daily adventure. What a wonderful thing it is to grow up and discover how really near to us God has always been!!!

Living in the Truth

Paul adds to all of this by saying we should live in the truth of God's will (verses 14-15). When a football running back breaks through the line, it is important that he avoid the tacklers. However, if he is not carrying the ball, it really does him no good to run. The same is true regarding our spiritual growth process. It is important that we avoid the lies Satan has thrown out to deceive us. But, if we do not stand firm on the truth of God, we really have not accomplished a great deal. In John 8:32 Jesus says the truth "will set you free." That is good news for Christians who are bound by emptiness. It is welcome relief for those who have been struggling with a snag in their spiritual development. There are two important aspects of the truth to which God wants us to hold. First, we must remember who we are and why we are here. This refers back to the previous point. You and I need to be totally dissatisfied with who we are if there are changes to be made. We cannot afford the luxury of throwing up our hands in despair and saying, "God, I give up. You will just have to take me like I am." God's calling is not for wimps! He tells us to "put to death the deeds of the body." James makes it quite clear that pure religion in the eyes of God involves "keeping oneself from being polluted by the world" (James 1:27). If I am still spotted in some way and I am truly thirsting for God, I will not rest until I have completely turned that problem over to Him! This does not mean people who thirst for God do not sin. It simply means they are not satisfied to let sin stay in their lives.

Remembering who we are also involves staying close to God. I must depend upon Him for everything. I must follow wherever He leads me. Paul says, "I want to *know* Christ and the power of his resurrection . . ." (Philippians 3:10, emphasis added). Peter says, "Christ suffered for you . . . that you should *follow* in his steps" (1 Peter 2:21). Paul also said, "For to me, to *live* is Christ . . ." (Philippians 1:21). Finally, Peter says it is a great privilege to *suffer and die* for Jesus (1 Peter 4:12-16). If you put all of these passages together, you find that staying close to God involves knowing Jesus, following Jesus, living for Jesus, suffering for Jesus, and possibly even dying for Jesus. Now, where are those people who claim God does not expect us to be fanatics? This description of devotion sounds pretty fanatical to me. Living in the truth of God's will demands that we remember who we are and why we are here.

It also demands that we remember our function in the body of Christ. In Ephesians 4:16 Paul describes our role in the body by talking about the ligaments which are joined together with each doing its own work. This is a very graphic and accurate description of our function together in the body of Jesus. There are no "one-man shows" in the church. There are no unimportant members of the body. We function best as a body only when every member is doing his/her part (1 Corinthians 12:26-27). Sometimes we do not recognize this simple truth. Many are like the guy who had just thrown an old Bible away. When a friend, who collected old books, heard about it, he threw a fit. "What kind of Bible was it? When was it published? Who published it?" he asked. "I don't remember," came the reply, "it was printed by Guten something or other." This really got the collector in a lather. "You idiot," he said, "you have thrown away one of the first books ever printed. A copy recently sold for $400,000." "Mine would not have been worth a dime," the friend said, "some clown named Martin Luther had scribbled all over it." Some people just do not recognize value when they see it, do they? Some Christians don't either. They look at their role in the body, and they feel they are totally insignificant and unimportant. Little do they know how truly valuable they are and how powerfully God can use them in combination with other Christians in the body. This is a basic truth to which God wants us to hold fast. Growing up in the Lord demands it.

It is certainly true that growing up can be quite an experience. In Ephesians 4, Paul shows us that filling up with Jesus is directly tied to growing up in the Lord. But growing up can be really frightening. After all, it means we have to turn away from our old comfortable ways and adopt new ways.

It was during the days of World War II. At a pivotal point of history in 1940, Winston Churchill said, "Let us . . . brace ourselves to our duty, and so bear ourselves that, if the British Empire and all its Commonwealth last for a thousand years, men will still say, 'This was their finest hour.'" When we face the challenge of growing spiritually with this triumphant attitude, we will feel our God-shaped hole beginning to fill up!!!

43

Discussion Questions

1. What relationship is there between "filling up" and "growing up"?

2. What specific changes will growing up spiritually have on our lives?

3. What kind of "lies" are spread in our society today?

4. Why do many feel their relationship with God is OK even though they are in rebellion to Him? What are some specific examples of this?

5. Describe the "bootstrap mentality" in your own words?

6. Why is it so difficult for some people to give God credit for things that happen in their lives?

7. Why is it important for us to be able to talk about what God is doing for us?

8. What does knowing who we are and where we are going demand of us?

9. How can you contribute to the welfare of the congregation where you worship?

Chapter 6
New Warfare

One night, a young lady found her husband standing over their baby's crib. She silently watched him as he gazed down at the sleeping infant. She saw on his face a mixture of emotions: disbelief, delight, amazement, enchantment and skepticism. She was touched by this unusual display of emotion. With her eyes glistening, she slipped her arms around her husband and said, "A penny for your thoughts." "It's just amazing," he replied, "I do not see how anybody can make a crib like that for only $46.50."

Sometimes we are about as deep as the shallow end of a wading pool. There are times when we realize just how shallow (empty) we are in our souls as well. We crave to be filled, but only God can fill the empty place inside our hearts. In Ephesians 5:5-21 Paul discusses the principles of light and darkness. God desires for us to get completely out of the darkness and fully into the light. In response to this, many attempt to gradually edge out of darkness, but they do not get fully into the light. They linger in the shadows! At work, they are not negligent in doing their job, but they make no real impact for Jesus either. They just do their job. In the family, they do not actively drive their children away from Jesus, but they do not lift up Jesus either. They just raise their family. On vacation, they do not do sinful things, but they also do not enjoy any deep communion with God. They just enjoy themselves. At the movies, they do not go to X-rated films, but they do not see G-rated films either. They stick with the R-rated movies. In their community, they do not participate in sin, but they do not reprove sin either. They just mind their own business.

Ephesians 5 says that "living in the shadows" is an extremely emptying lifestyle. God wants us to get completely out of darkness (verses 7-8). He wants us to wake up from our spiritual sleep (verse 14) and actively oppose the forces of darkness all around us (verse

11). You cannot do these things from the shadows. You have to get all the way into the light. When we do that, God will fill us up with His Holy Spirit (verse 18). When that happens, we are never quite the same again. We begin changing in ways we never dreamed possible, and the fullness just continues to consume us. But, what specifically does the Spirit do in filling us up? That is the question which we address in this chapter.

Inward Changes

Few passages describe the inner workings of God's Spirit better than Galatians 5. In verses 16-17 Paul tells us the Spirit of God and the desires of the flesh fight against one another. Only one of those forces can be the dominant influence of your life. The desires of the flesh (verses 19-21) have a real emptying impact on the human heart. You cannot try to hold onto any of those things and expect God's Spirit to fill you up. You have to get away from the thoughts and desires of the flesh. This clearly includes the sinful ways of the world, but it is not limited to that. We are talking about wholesale rejection of the world's ways. The attitude of the world is, "You have to get what you can get anyway you can get it without worrying about who you have to step on." The priorities of the world say you have to pay your bills, get ahead on your job, keep up with your friends in the race to accumulate things, drive a nice car, live in a nice house, and the list goes on and on. Christians who want to be filled with God's Spirit cannot get tangled up in this lifestyle. The world defines success in terms of yearly salary, power, prestige and popularity. God's Spirit has a totally different definition of success.

I used to install underground sprinkling systems. First, we dug the ditches and then we laid the pipe. When we went down the line connecting the pipes together, it was inevitable that dirt would get inside. When we finished the job and got ready to attach the spray nozzles, we had to get the dirt out of the pipes. We turned on the water and watched as the first stream sprayed out. The water would be dark brown with all of the dirt and rocks that had gotten inside the pipes. As the water continued to flow, it gradually became lighter and lighter until all the dirt was gone and we were left with a crystal clear stream.

Titus 3 describes the work of the Spirit inside our hearts in much the same way. Paul says God's children experience a "washing of regeneration and renewal of the Holy Spirit." That happens when we become a Christian and the dirt begins flowing out of our lives. The "washing" continues until the "dirt" becomes lighter and lighter. As we continue allowing the Spirit to fill us up, we are eventually left with a crystal clear life that is continually being renewed.

This whole process is described as a "change" in 2 Corinthians 3:18. It is a change which is brought about "by the Spirit of the Lord." The word for "change" in this verse comes from a word which means "metamorphosis." Obviously, this refers to a radical alteration which begins on the inside and continues until it emerges on the outside. Galatians 5:22-24 fills in the blanks by mentioning specific qualities of character the Spirit gives us. Paul ends that context in verse 25 where he says, "Since we live by the Spirit, let us keep in step with the Spirit." Walking in the Spirit touches every thought we think, every attitude we have, and every decision we make. Keeping in step with the Spirit reaches down to the deepest recesses of our souls and moves us completely out of the darkness. You cannot be filled with the Spirit by attempting to live "in the shadows."

Outward Results

Ephesians 5:18 gives a striking contrast. First, it says we should not "get drunk on wine." Now, everyone knows what happens when a person gets drunk (or, is filled) with wine. It alters his speech, his judgment, his reasoning and everything else about him. Being "filled with the Spirit" has much the same impact. In verses 19-21 Paul gives a listing of changes that will overtake us when we are filled with the Spirit.

First, being filled with the Spirit will cause us to overflow in song (verse 19). The "psalms and hymns and spiritual songs" are all songs of praise and adoration to God. So, the songs that pass over our lips actually spring from the well of our heart which is filled with joy, peace, and eternal hope. Now, be sure to get this point — singing is not a commandment in this verse. Nowhere in this context is there the slightest hint of a requirement that must be fulfilled within given specifications. Singing is a natural result of being filled with the Spirit. It can happen anytime without warning. You could be sitting at your desk or taking a walk and suddenly break out into a song. That is the way it happens when you are filled up — it just naturally spills out. It is totally inappropriate to force Ephesians 5:19 into the mold of a worship assembly. You can read Ephesians 5 frontwards, backwards and sideways and you will not find the slightest reference to an assembly. Paul is talking about the singing that takes place in the life of a Christian who is overflowing with the Spirit of God. It just happens! You cannot schedule it. You cannot fit it onto a program of worship. Singing as described in this verse is a spontaneous action that springs from the joy of being filled up with God.

Second, being filled with the Spirit will cause us to be grateful to God in all circumstances (verse 20). Most of the times of our lives can be easily divided into two categories — good times and bad times. In the good times, the gratitude we feel toward God comes from a recognition of the many blessings He continually showers upon us. It comes very naturally to have these feelings during good times. We do not need a great deal of help from God's Spirit in this area. However, the bad times come around sooner or later, and we are still expected to be grateful. That is when it gets a little tough. But, because we are filled with God's Spirit, we can still be grateful. Certainly, God does not expect us to be happy about tragedy. When something tragic takes place in your life and you are in the depths of heartache and grief, it is very natural and totally appropriate for you to be down and discouraged. However, God's Spirit works within us to maintain a grateful spirit even in these times. This gratitude springs from a continued recognition of God's blessings in other areas of our lives. It also comes from the faith-rooted recognition that God is in control, and He will bring all things together for the good eventually. What a wonderful gift that is! When the rest of the world would feel bitterness and resentment, we are able to overflow in gratitude and praise. When everyone else would be drowning in self-pity and anger, we are able to rise out of those feelings with a heart filled with thanksgiving and confidence. That is what happens in the life of a person who is filled up with God's Spirit!

Finally, being filled with the Spirit will cause us to be submissive to one another (verse 21). You know, it is not easy to submit to someone. It goes against our nature to humble ourselves. Most people are much more comfortable in the driver's seat. But, the Spirit of God within us makes it possible for us to overcome that nature and to have a submissive attitude in our dealings with others. This submission is not connected to a feeling of respect or regard for the other person. If that were the motivation, we would not be submissive to those for whom we had no respect. Submission to others comes primarily from a submission to the Lordship of Jesus Christ. I may not like you at all. You may be arrogant and self-centered in your relationship to me. But, I am still supposed to have an attitude of submission toward you because that is what my Lord wants me to do. So, my submission to you has nothing to do with who *you* are. It has everything to do with who *Jesus* is.

It is true that sometimes our spiritual perception does not run extremely deep. In fact, at times we run on dead empty. At those times God wants to fill us up. Ephesians 5 shows that being filled with God is directly connected to being filled with His Spirit. Henry Drummond once said, "The pearl diver lives at the bottom of the ocean by means of the pure air conveyed to him from above. His life is entirely dependent on the breath from above. We are down here, like the diver, to gather pearls for our Master's crown. The source of our life comes from the life-giving Spirit." What a wonderful way of expressing the effect of God's Spirit in our lives!

The fullness of our God-shaped hole depends upon whether or not we are filled with God's Spirit. We can "quench the Spirit" (1 Thessalonians 5:19). We do this through continuing to walk according to the wisdom and ways of the world. We can also do it by refusing to acknowledge the work of the Spirit in our lives. When we do either of these things, we put a crimp in the hose that God uses to fill us up. Like the diver, we can live for a brief moment of time without that supply of "breath from above." Navy Seals can hold their breath for up to 3 minutes. Have you ever tried to hold your breath for that long? That is truly an amazing feat! But, there is something even more amazing — a Christian who lives his life without allowing the Spirit of God to influence him. You cannot go through life "holding your breath" and still have a sense of fullness and joy. You have to let God fill you up!

Discussion Questions

1. Why do some Christians attempt to edge out of darkness and stay in the shadows instead of getting completely into the light?

2. Can you think of any specific examples of this?

3. What types of inward changes does the Spirit produce within us?

4. In what specific ways does He help us to become more like Jesus?

5. What types of outward results does the Spirit produce in our lives?

6. Why is singing a natural result of being filled with the Spirit?

7. In what situations is it most difficult to maintain our gratitude to God?

8. Define meekness in your own words.

Chapter 7
New Clothing

When confusion enters a conversation, some humorous things can happen. A preacher was being interviewed by a search committee for a pulpit position. The committee asked him what his favorite section of Scripture was. He answered,

> Once upon a time, a man went from Jerusalem to Jericho and fell among thieves. The thieves threw him into the weeds and the weeds grew up and choked that man. He then went on and met the Queen of Sheba and she gave that man one thousand talents of gold and silver and a hundred changes of raiment. He got in his chariot and drove furiously to the Red Sea. When he got there, the waters parted and he drove to the other side. On the other side, he drove under an olive tree and got his hair caught on a limb that was hanging down. He hung there many days and many nights, and the ravens brought him food to eat and water to drink. One night while he was hanging there asleep, his wife, Delilah, came along and cut off his hair, and he dropped and fell on the stony ground. The children of a nearby city came up and said, "Go up, thou bald head," and the man cursed and two she-bears came out of the woods and tore up the children. Then it began to rain, and it rained for 40 days and 40 nights. He went and hid in a cave. Later he went out and invited a man to join him for a feast. The man declined because he had just married a wife, so he went out to the highways and byways and compelled others to come. Then he went to Jericho and blew his trumpet 7 times and the walls fell down. As he walked by one of the damaged buildings, he saw Queen Jezebel sitting high up in a window. When she saw him, she laughed and made fun of him. The man became furious and said, "Toss her down," and they did. Then he said, "Toss her down again," and they did. They threw her down seventy times seven. And the fragments they gathered were 12 baskets full. The question now is, "Whose wife shall she be in the resurrection?"

When the preacher left the interview, one of the committee members said, "He is a little long-winded, isn't he?" Another committee member answered, "Yes, but doesn't he know his Bible well!"

Sometimes confusion can be quite humorous. At those times it is harmless and easily resolved. But, there are times when confusion revolves around spiritual matters. At these times, it can be very damaging (even deadly). Throughout the book of Ephesians, Paul tells us the variety of ways in which God wants to fill us up. In Chapter 6 he sums it all up by saying, "Put on the full armor of God." The term, "put on" means "to be enveloped in or to hide in." The phrase "the armor of God" is explained with words like truth, righteousness, faith, etc. These are clearly inward traits. So, the concept with which Paul ends this letter is the same one he has emphasized throughout the rest of the book — being filled up with God on the inside.

If you are like me, you may be wondering why we need this armor. After all, we live in a country in which there is little religious persecution. We are free to practice our religion without fear of interference from the government. But, if you are thinking this way, you are completely missing the point. We are not doing battle with the government or any other human being. Verse 12 makes it crystal-clear that our fight is against the spiritual forces of darkness. That is the bad news, and it gets much worse. Verse 11 mentions "the schemes of the devil." You see, you may take life as it comes without giving a second thought to it, but Satan does not approach life that way. He is out to get you, and he knows the areas in which you are the most vulnerable. That is where his "schemes" come in. Satan has a strategic plan for his attack on you. He knows what he is doing today, and he knows where he plans to hit you tomorrow. If you are living life in a haphazard manner, you are a prime target for his attacks. Verse 13 mentions "the evil day." There are many evil days in a Christian's life. Any day you do battle with Satan is "an evil day." It may be over the hospital bed of a loved one. It may be in an unemployment office. It may be in a dark room when you are by yourself, but the evil day always comes! When it does, it is vital that you be filled up with God!

When we are filled up with God, it will result in —
1. Spiritual Strength
2. Opposing Satan
3. Standing Our Ground

Spiritual Strength

Paul says we must be strong "in the Lord and in the power of His might." I am really glad Paul put that in there. If God is depending upon me to be strong in my own strength against Satan, I am sunk. But, if Jesus is with me to be my strength, I can make it. Many times we blame it on a lack of will power when we fall to temptation. On the other side, we tend to boast about our will power when we win over some enticement. The truth is, our own will power has nothing whatever to do with our fight against Satan. If you meet him on the battlefield of your life and all you are carrying is your will power, "you are in a heap of trouble." It is only through the power and strength of Jesus Christ that we are able to overcome Satan. That is why it is essential for us to be filled up with Jesus.

Imagine a big body builder whose small son is trying to impress his father. The boy comes into the room flexing his muscles and wanting his daddy to feel them. He lifts a 10 pound object over his head, and his face beams with pride as his father applauds with approval. That boy's father can lift much more weight than 10 pounds, but he is humoring his son. Sometimes I think that is the way God is. We approach our lives in our own strength. It is almost like we are trying to show God how strong we can be. He looks at us with longing in His eyes because He can do so much more through us than we can ever do on our own. God is willing to fill us with His power as we face Satan "in the evil day."

Opposing Satan

In verse 13 Paul says he wants us to "withstand" in the evil day. That word literally means, "to oppose or to resist." As we saw in the previous point, this is only possible through the power and strength of Jesus Christ. Peter tells us that angels are much stronger and more powerful than human beings (2 Peter 2:11). Since Satan is an angelic being, it is obvious he has no reason to fear us. However, with God at our side, Satan has every reason in the world to tremble in fear. We saw it happen quite literally as Jesus walked the earth. Any time Jesus confronted a demon, the demon quaked and pleaded with Jesus not to hurt him. It is true — at the name of Jesus, "the devils believe and tremble" (James 2:19).

There are two movies that come to my mind when I think of our battle against Satan. The first movie is *Rocky*. That was the story of an underdog boxer who was given the chance to fight for the heavyweight championship of the world. He worked out and trained tirelessly until he got strong and fit enough to win the title. What a wonderfully inspiring story! It was so inspiring that people bought memberships in health clubs all across our country. Wouldn't it be great if this were the story of our fight against Satan! Don't you wish that you could get up early and begin training so that, when you met Satan, you could be strong and fit enough to whip him? That would be great — if it were reality. The truth is, it does not work that way.

The truth of our fight against Satan is more like a movie called, *My Bodyguard*. This was the story of a small boy who was constantly being bullied at school. Eventually, the boy hired a larger kid in the school to be his bodyguard and to protect him from the bullies. That is the way it really is as we face Satan. We are small and frail in comparison to him, and he could chew us up in one bite. But he won't dare touch us as long as "our bodyguard" is near us.

Satan does not feel comfortable in the same room with God. In fact, if God is very close by, Satan will run away (James 4:7). So, it is really important for us to walk very closely to God. Unfortunately, Satan feels very much at home in the lives of many Christians. He can tell the difference between a person who is genuinely full of God and one who is simply full of hot air. The first person will oppose Satan and win while the other spends his life in a futile and failing struggle.

Standing Our Ground

Verse 13 uses another word that we need to examine closely. He ends the verse by telling us to "stand." That word means that we should never lose our footing. People who stand up for God have always been "like a tree planted by streams of water" (Psalm 1:3). Paul gives this same description to Christians in Colossians 2:6-7. Trees are amazing things! Storms can come and winds can blow and the tree will bend almost to the ground. But when the storm passes, the tree continues to stand where it stood before. You see, trees have root systems which hold them securely in the ground. That is how we are when we are filled up with Jesus. Psalm 1:4 gives a stark contrast when it describes ungodly people. David says those people are "like chaff that the wind blows away." What is the difference between these two types of people? Why are some able to stand firmly while others are driven by the wind?

Have you ever seen a football game in which the running back gets the ball and runs headlong into the defensive line? Sometimes the running back hits the line and stops dead in his tracks for no gain. Other times he hits the line and carries a defensive lineman about five yards down the field. That is how it is in our spiritual battle. Satan is the running back, and we are the linemen. Sometimes Satan hits us with something, and he stops dead in his tracks without having any affect on us at all. Other times, he hits us and carries us all the way to the other end of the field. What is the difference in us at these times? Why are we strong at times and so very weak at others? The determining factor is how full we are of Jesus! If you have not been spending much time with Jesus, and Satan hits you, you are in for quite a ride before he is through with you. But, if you spend time in prayer, meditation, study and doing all the things Paul describes in the book of Ephesians, your God-shaped hole will fill up, and you will stand firmly when Satan comes to call on you.

Imagine two eighteen-wheelers driving south on a freeway with a strong wind blowing out of the west. It does not take two seconds to determine which one is empty and which has a full load. The full one is stable and holds the road firmly. You might think twice about passing the empty one. Sometimes when we are empty, we endanger not only ourselves, but everyone around us!

Spiritual emptiness is a deadly thing. There are various levels of emptiness. Every child of God experiences the roller coaster of being empty at one moment and being full the next. Keeping our God-shaped hole full is a task which requires daily attention. We cannot go through life neglecting this essential area and expecting ourselves to remain spiritually healthy and energetic. It simply does not work that way.

The ocean contains many fascinating creatures. One such animal is the stone fish. When the stone fish stings, it brings about an excruciatingly high level of pain. The victim has no doubt that something terrible has happened to him. He may cry out, lose consciousness, and even die.

Another fascinating ocean creature is the sea snake. Many varieties of sea snakes produce no pain when they bite. Their poison works slowly and subtly. The victim begins to feel sluggish as his body begins to shut down. Eventually he goes into what appears to be a deep sleep. However, he is not asleep — he is simply unable to move. Many times the person never revives.

When you apply the effects of these two creatures to our spiritual existence, some interesting things become clear. Some sins have a very obvious and immediate impact on us. From the moment we become involved in it, we know we are in trouble. If we do not make some corrections, we will die spiritually in a very short time. However, spiritual emptiness is more like the sea snake. It slowly and unnoticeably creeps into our heart. It comes from being too busy to tend to our spiritual lives. It comes from putting material things ahead of our souls. It comes from a variety of different things, but it always comes. When our God-shaped hole is empty, we have two options. We can continue to take care of our own affairs of life and let our relationship with God be destroyed. On the other hand, we can get our priorities right, spend time with God before we do anything else and watch as God takes care of the rest! What a wonderful God we serve! How precious it is to be filled up with Him!!!

Discussion Questions

1. Describe the armor that God wants us to wear.

2. How does "filling the God-shaped hole" apply to the armor that Paul discusses?

3. What is the difference between relying on our own strength and relying on God's strength?

4. In what specific ways can we oppose Satan?

5. Why is it important to distinguish between the *Rocky* mentality and the *My Bodyguard* mentality? Which do you have most often? Why?

6. In what specific ways are Christians like "a tree planted by streams of water?"

Section
Two

Section 2
Running to God

Once the football player quenches his thirst, he is ready to do what he came to do — play the game. You see, a football player does not put on his pads, practice two times a day in the scorching heat, and go through all kinds of pain and discomfort just so he can stand on the sideline and drink Gatorade. He is there to play the game. However, there are times when his performance in the game is improved by taking time out periodically to quench his thirst.

That is the way it is with us. We are not here to stand on the sideline and "quench our thirst" for God. We are here to serve Him and to draw nearer to Him in many very special ways. However, our ability to draw nearer to God is hindered when we are spiritually empty. For that reason, we must give attention to our spiritual thirst before we can draw nearer to God. There is nothing more terrifying than being alone and feeling that no one knows or cares about you in any way. The world is filled with people who live in this fear every day. Christians should never have this problem. God has taken steps to make it possible for us to draw near and stay close to "His precious, bleeding side." Let's take some time to consider some of these things and the effect they will have on our everyday lives!

Chapter 8
Getting on the Road

A man who was known for having a bad temper was playing golf with his preacher. After missing three straight putts on the edge of the cup, the man exploded, "I missed! I missed! How could I miss?!!!" With that, he slung his putter into a lake, kicked the side of the golf cart, and threw his fist into a tree. The preacher looked at the man and said, "Don't you know that God doesn't like us to show our anger like that? You better watch out, because there are angels whose only job is to search out people who lose their temper, and strike them with lightning." The man was embarrassed, and acted much better on the next few holes. But, on the last three holes, his putts missed just slightly to the left. When the last one veered off the cup, the man went into another tirade, "I missed! How could I miss?!!!" Having said that, he broke his putter across his knee and threw it as far as he could. Suddenly, the sky grew dark when an ominous cloud gathered over their heads. There was a tremendous thunder and a bolt of lightning came down and hit the preacher who was standing beside the angry man. A ghostly silence overcame the golf course. Suddenly the silence was broken by a small voice from the sky saying, "I missed! I missed! I can't believe I missed!"

There are many times when we miss what we are trying to hit. In the spiritual realm, missing our target is called "sin." The natural result of sin is separation from God. From the first sin of the first human being, God has been extremely concerned about closing this gap to make it possible for us to draw closer to Him once more. In spite of God's concerns, many human beings are completely unaware of their need to draw near to Him. They remain blinded to the way made available to them by God. Many are like the people God describes in Psalm 32:9 where He says, "Do not be like the horse or the mule, which have no understanding but must be controlled by bit and bridle or they will not come to you." Clearly, some humans are just like a stubborn mule when it comes to drawing nearer to God. In this section, we will notice some specific means of drawing nearer to the Lord. But before we do that, we need to start at the very beginning to discover the plan God set in motion to solve the problem of man's separation from Him.

In considering the process of drawing nearer to God, we see God designing the plan, Jesus executing it, and man responding to it.

God Designing the Plan

As soon as Adam and Eve took a bite out of the fruit, God set His plan into motion. In Genesis 3:15 He tells Satan that a day is coming when the Redeemer will break the death grip that Satan has on mankind. What a wonderful promise! Isn't it great to know God cares so much about us? A single day did not pass before the wheels of our deliverance began turning. Once God saw our need to draw closer to Him, He sent a part of Himself to the Earth to pave the road.

In Hebrews 10:5-10 a beautiful picture is painted of Jesus going into the throne room of His Father and offering to be the sacrifice for all mankind. He uses the phrase "I have come to do your will, O God" two separate times in this passage. So, from the very time man sinned, God designed a plan to bring us closer to Him. Only He could come up with the plan. You and I were in no position to negotiate. The gavel had sounded and the verdict had been handed down: Guilty as charged! The penalty for our crime was eternal death. There was no logical reason for God to desire us to draw nearer to Him. But then, love never makes sense. We do things for people we love that do not seem to make one bit of sense to those who are looking on. But everything makes sense to the one who is in love. That was God's predicament. He was head over heels in love with us. The day we decided to walk away from Him was the day He was compelled to keep the road of return open to us. Can you imagine an all-powerful God being compelled to do something? What on earth could be powerful enough to force the Creator's hand? Only love has that kind of power! For God so loved the world that He designed a marvelous plan for us to draw near to Him!

Jesus Executing the Plan

Once Jesus set foot on the earth and began his preaching ministry, it became apparent He was here for a reason. Jesus discussed His role in God's plan on many occasions. In John 14:6 He says, "I am the way and the truth and the life." In other words, Jesus is the road that God paved for us to draw near to Him. There is no other road. All other paths are blockaded with the sign "Bridge Out Ahead" posted in plain view. You can take other roads, but you just have to turn around and start over, because they do not lead anywhere.

In San Jose, California, there is a house called the Winchester Mansion. This magnificent place was built by the widow of the man who invented the Winchester rifle. She was so guilt-ridden about all the people who had died because of her husband's invention, she began imagining all of those spirits haunting her. In order to confuse the spirits, she would add secret chambers onto the house periodically. She built doorways that opened into brick walls. Elaborate stairways which led nowhere were scattered throughout the house. She did all of this in an attempt to escape the spirits that haunted her mind. Mrs. Winchester is gone, but the house remains as a monument to her insanity. Who on earth would want to have a house with doorways and staircases that do not lead anywhere? But, that is exactly what people do when they try to approach God without Jesus.

Jesus became a little more specific about His role in God's plan in John 12:32-33. He told His disciples He was going to be "lifted up from the earth." The final statement in verse 33 shows He was talking about His death on the cross. Jesus said the result of being "lifted up" would be that all men would be "drawn to Him." There it is! All men would be drawn to Jesus by His death on the cross. That was Jesus' role in God's plan.

Paul tells us Jesus fulfilled that role perfectly. In Ephesians 2:13 Paul says ". . . in Christ Jesus you who once were far away have been brought near through the blood of Christ." Later, in verse 18,

He tells us that "through him we both have access to the Father." So, God *designed* the road for us to travel as we draw near to Him. Jesus' purpose was to *be* the road which provides access to God.

There was a little boy who owned a toy sail boat. He built it from some wood in his daddy's shop. He was playing with it in the lake one day when the wind carried it away. The boy was heartbroken to lose the toy he had made with his own hands. A few days later, he was walking by a toy store, and he saw the boat in the window. He rushed into the store, and asked the price of the boat. The boy dug into his pockets, slapped his money on the counter, grabbed his toy boat, and left. Upon leaving the shop, the boy was heard saying, "Now, you are twice mine. I built you and then I lost you. But now I have bought you back."

Doesn't that describe what Jesus did for us? John 1:1-3 says He "built us." When we chose to sin against His will, we became lost (Romans 6:23). On that day, Jesus began a frantic search for us. In order for us to have a marker to guide us back to the Father, He crawled up on the cross and died. That cross serves as the lighthouse for those who are lost in the ocean of sin and are trying to find their way back to the Lord. Jesus fulfilled His role in the Father's plan perfectly.

Man Responding to the Plan

God designed the road and Jesus is the road. Now it is up to you and me to walk on that road back to God. Hebrews 10:22 says, "let us draw near" to God. The rest of the New Testament tells us how to do that. John 1:12 says those who believe in Jesus as God's beloved Son have "the right to become children of God." So, belief in Jesus is the first step down the road. In Acts 3:19 Peter tells us to "repent, then, and turn to God . . . ." The word "repent" is self explanatory. But there is a phrase attached to that word that is interesting — "turn to God." Before we can "turn to God" we must have turned away from God. We did this when we sinned. But when we turn to God, that is a move to draw closer to Him. We do this when we repent. So, belief and repentance are two essential elements in starting down the road of return to God. Galatians 3:27 says those who have been baptized into Christ have put on Christ.

Of course, getting "into Christ" and "putting on Christ" are two ways of referring to drawing nearer to Christ. You cannot get into something or put on something without automatically getting closer to it. But how do we get into Christ according to Galatians 3? We are baptized into Christ!

So, there you have it. God designed the road, Jesus is the road and we step onto the road through belief, repentance and baptism. Now, how can we be certain that we have reasoned correctly in this regard? Turn back to Hebrews 10. Remember, verse 22 tells us to "draw near" to God. Well, keep on reading. This verse mentions three things. First, it mentions "assurance of faith." That is belief. Then it talks about "hearts sprinkled to cleanse us from a guilty conscience." That describes the act of repentance in the human heart. Finally, it refers to "bodies washed with pure water." Now, what other function does water have in our journey back to God other than in baptism? So, whether you read throughout the New Testament, or whether you limit your study to Hebrews 10, the message is the same. If we are going to travel the road that leads nearer to God, we have to step on it through belief, repentance and baptism. Once we have done that, the delightful journey begins.

Separation from God is the problem. Sin is the cause. God, in His wisdom, is the only solution. Before we look closely at how we can draw nearer to God, it is essential that we understand these things. When General Motors wants to build a new car, the process begins in the board room where the executives and engineers decide to put a new design in the product line. Once that decision is made, it is passed down to the managers of the individual plants. The managers work feverishly along with their individual craftsmen to come up with a new design. Once approved by the executive board, the design along with all of its specifications goes down to the assembly line workers who actually build the car. If there is a breakdown in any of these three levels, the entire process comes to a screeching halt and the result is, no new car!

The plan to make it possible for us to draw nearer to God works this same way. God designed the plan (board room). He passed it down to Jesus who implemented the plan (manager at the plant). It is our job to actually walk down the road that leads us nearer to God (assembly line workers). Like GM, if there is a breakdown at any of these three levels, the entire process comes to a screeching halt and the result is, no nearness to God. However, unlike GM, there is only one possible level for the plan to breakdown. God has already flawlessly designed the plan. Jesus has already fully implemented the plan. The only level remaining is ours. If you are not drawing nearer to God, it may be because you have not taken the first step down the road. Some have gotten onto the road, but they have pulled over, and have been sitting on the shoulder for a while. Drawing nearer to God cannot be done from a sit down position! God has designed and paved the road. Now, it's your move!

Discussion Questions

1. What is the basic difference between filling up with God and drawing nearer to Him?

2. What has God done to make it possible for us to draw nearer to Him?

3. What was Jesus' role in executing that plan?

4. Now that Jesus has executed the plan, what specific blessings do we receive?

5. What is involved in our response to God's plan to draw nearer to Him?

Chapter 9
Staying in My Lane

An American woman who was visiting China found a curious looking medallion. She bought it and wore it to every social function she attended. It was a great conversation starter as well as a very attractive piece of jewelry. But there was a Chinese inscription on it which she could not read. She attended a diplomatic dinner in Washington where she met the Chinese ambassador. She noticed him looking at the medallion with a faint grin on his face. She asked him, "Have you seen one of these before?" The ambassador admitted that he had, and then he changed the subject abruptly. The woman asked, "Would you please translate this inscription for me?" He said he would rather not. But the woman continued to insist. The ambassador finally agreed. "Very well," he replied, "it says 'Licensed Prostitute, City of Shanghai.'"

There are many things in this world which are interesting and harmless. God has arranged His creation so that we can have happy and enjoyable lives while we are here. However, there are some things in this world which make it impossible for us to draw nearer to God. 1 Thessalonians 1:9 tells how the Thessalonians "turned to God from idols." If you look carefully in that phrase, you will find two different turns. It specifically says they turned to God. That is equivalent to drawing nearer to God. But before they could do that, they had to turn away from idols. Idols and God simply do not fit in the same life. There are some things in this world from which we must turn away completely if we want to draw nearer to God.

James 4:8 assures us that, if we will draw nearer to God, He will draw nearer to us. Upon further study, we find that verse 8 is in the middle of a context (verses 4-10) which very strongly instructs us to draw away from the world. Now, there are two basic reactions to that. Some people have gone to the extreme of getting themselves so completely separate from the world that they have totally isolated themselves. One of the purposes of monasteries is to get the monks away from the polluting influences of the world. In John 17:15-16 Jesus makes a clear distinction between being *in* the world and being *of* the world. You see, God placed us in this world. He does not expect or even desire us to be completely separate from the world. After all, it was Jesus who said, "Go into all the world and preach the good news . . ." (Mark 16:15). He would not have told us to go into the world if he desired us to separate ourselves from the world.

Having said that, God also does not desire us to be so secular that there is no difference between us and the world. Romans 12:2 makes it quite plain that we must not be "conformed" to the world. That word literally means "to be pressed into a mold." God does not expect us to be like the world in the sense that we look exactly like it in everything we do. So, there has to be a happy medium between being totally separate and being completely secular. In this chapter we will try to find that happy medium.

As we draw nearer to God, we must draw away from —

The Ways of the World

At this particular point, we will not discuss the sinful ways of the world. That discussion is done in the next segment. The point right here is that the world has some non-sinful lifestyle practices which make it impossible for us to draw nearer to God. In James 4:4-6 the Holy Spirit inspired James to use some of the strongest language in the Bible to say we should not be friends of the world. That does not mean we should not make friends of people in the world. It means we should not become overly friendly with the ways and the lifestyles of the world. Why would God feel so strongly about this? We are given a little insight into that question when we read Exodus 19:3-6. God is explaining to Moses that He delivered Israel from their bondage in Egypt so they could be a "treasured possession" to Him. In other words, God wanted them to be His people in a special way. Things have not changed much when you come to the New Testament. Titus 2:14 tells us that Jesus died on the cross so He could have "a people that are his very own." God really wants us to be His. That applies to many specific areas of our lives. First, it applies to our job selections. When people of the world look for a job, what are the first questions they ask? Well, they want to know about the salary. They want to know something about the benefits and the possibilities of advancement. Most people focus on the working conditions as well as the retirement plans. Christians are concerned about these things. However, these should not be the first concerns of God's children. Christians should ask about opportunities to serve Jesus while on the job. They should ask if there will be enough time left for them to worship God publicly and to enjoy their own private communion with God. They should investigate whether there will be enough time for them to lead their families to Jesus.

When it comes to dating and marriage, the world focuses on looks, education, family background, financial status, career plans and common interests. Before looking at these things, Christians should ask if the person loves the Lord. They need to be sure that the person is a student of God's word and is committed to Jesus Christ as the Lord of his life.

Sometimes it is necessary to relocate ourselves and our families. When that happens, the world wants to know about the job opportunities and the cost of living. In addition, they want to know about the quality of the community, banking services, and schools. Christians should also ask about the opportunities to serve God in the community. They should investigate the church there to see if it is Spirit-led or spiritually dead. They should ask about their opportunities for involvement in the work of the church in that location.

These are only a few areas in which we are called to make some decisions. It is clear that the world's questions are necessary and important. Being a Christian does not mean you do not care about any of the issues the world raises. However, it does mean that you ask the first questions first. If you are looking for a job, you first need to know whether you can work at that job and still do everything you need to do in your service to God. If the answer to that question is "yes," then you should ask about the money and the other issues. If the answer to that question is "no," then it does not matter how much money may be involved. When you are considering dating or marrying someone, you must find out whether the person will help you to draw nearer to God. If the answer is "yes," then you can consider all of the physical matters. If the answer is "no," then it does not matter how attractive or successful the person may be.

It is not that Christians do not care about financial and social success. On the contrary, Christians are some of the most ambitious people in the world. But it is possible to be ambitious, and still have your head on straight. It is possible to attain the success the world has to offer in terms of financial and career matters without having those things as your primary concern. When a person understands this and makes pleasing God his highest priority, he will begin drawing nearer to Him every day of his life.

The Practices of the World

If you read James 4:8-10, it is apparent that the Holy Spirit is encouraging us to turn away from the sinful practices of the world. In this area, people who are looking to justify their sinful lifestyles begin to say, "Show me in the Bible where it says I can't do this or that." We need to say two things about that attitude. First, these kind of people really do not care what the Bible says. If there was a "book, chapter and verse" which condemns their lifestyle, they would probably continue to live that way. Second, there usually is a specific verse in the Bible to condemn a certain activity. However, we really do not need a specific verse for every decision we make in this life. Let me explain.

The Bible teaches in general principles as well as in specific statements. In Philippians 1:27 we are told to live lives which are "worthy of the gospel." In Ephesians 4:1 we are told to "live a life worthy" of our calling. These passages are simply telling us to live lives which are appropriate for a child of God. In every culture on earth, there are things which Christians are expected to do. People everywhere expect a Christian to share, to love others, to forgive and to be kind. On the other hand, there are things which Christians are not expected to do in any culture. No one expects to find a Christian drinking, carousing, cursing, or wearing provocative clothing. These are only a few examples, and you could find a Bible passage to address most of them. But the point is, when you can't find such a passage, you need to apply another test to the activity in question: Would you be comfortable doing it if everyone there knew you were a Christian? If the answer to that question is "no," you do not need "book, chapter and verse" for you to know that activity is wrong.

The Appearance of the World

Throughout the Bible, God tells His people not to do certain things. Many of these things seem harmless to us, because we simply do not understand the culture of the time. For instance, in Deuteronomy 14:1 God tells Israel not to shave the front part of their head. With some of the hairstyles going around today, this one seems rather calm. Why would God not want His people to shave the front part of their head? There is nothing inherently wrong with that particular hairstyle, but there was a reason God did not want His children doing it. The reason is that in that day and time, the pagan priests wore those type of hairstyles as an identification mark for their particular idol. Even though there was nothing morally wrong with it, it identified God's people with a sinful element of their society, and God has never desired that.

We find the same thing in the New Testament. 1 Peter 3:3 says Christian women should not wear costly jewelry or braid their hair. Now, there is nothing wrong with braiding hair and wearing jewelry. However, in Peter's day, that was the appearance of the common prostitutes. Peter was saying it is completely inappropriate for a daughter of God to go around looking like a daughter of the devil.

Today, if you want to wear jewelry or shave the front part of your head, more power to you. These things have no sinful connotation whatsoever in our culture. However, there are some things which Christians today must avoid simply for the sake of appearance. For instance, wearing shirts or caps which display beer, liquor, or marijuana is totally out of place for a Christian. People who wear these articles of clothing do not necessarily get drunk or high. And there is certainly nothing wrong with wearing caps or T-shirts. The point is, these articles of clothing associate the people who wear them with a certain element of our society which is not right for a Christian. So, Christians should not wear them. Certain hairstyles today have the same problems attached to them. In addition to these things, some Christian teenagers proudly display obviously Satanic images on their clothes, on their walls at home, on their books at school and in the jewelry they wear. These things do not automatically make these young people Satan worshipers. However, they do associate them with that element in our society. Because of that, Christian young people should not display those images.

The list of these kinds of things is rather long, but the point is simple: there are things which are not wrong in and of themselves which Christians must still avoid because of the appearance. If a child of God is interested in drawing nearer to his Father, he has to draw away from the appearance of the world!

There is a tremendous struggle going on in the hearts of many Christians. They really want to serve God and to please Him in their lives, but they have some problems which make that impossible. Some cannot break away from the ways of the world. They look and act just like the world in the questions they ask and the priorities they have. Others are caught up in the sinful practices of the world and they cannot escape. Still others are struggling with the appearance of what they are doing. Well, it is time for the inner turmoil to end. There is only one way to make that happen, and that is to make a clear decision as to who is the Lord of your life. Once that question is answered, the struggle eases up. That is why Elijah challenged God's people to make a decision about who they were going to serve (1 Kings 18:21). If Baal was God, they needed to follow him. If Jehovah is God, then they should follow Him. The main thing was they needed to make a decision. This is the same decision which faces all of us today. Is Jehovah the Lord of our lives, or is someone else? It does not matter who the "someone else" may be. If it is anyone besides Jesus Christ, we have made the wrong choice. It is time for the game-playing to stop. It is time for the vacillating to be over. It is time for the testing of the water with your big toe to end. It is time to jump in and begin drawing nearer to God!

Discussion Questions

1. As we draw nearer to God, from what specific things might we need to draw away?

2. Why do we tend toward the extremes of either total separation from the world or complete secularism?

3. What are some of the nonsinful ways of the world which make it impossible for us to draw nearer to God?

4. Why do Christians tend to ask the same questions the world does rather than "asking the first questions first?"

5. What are some of the sinful practices of the world which make it impossible for us to draw nearer to God?

6. What are some general principles of Scripture which prescribe Christian conduct? To what specific situations would these principles apply?

7. What are some of the "appearances of the world" that Christians must avoid?

Chapter 10
Continuing Steadfastly

Paul Harvey tells the story of a college basketball coach who was upstairs shaving. His wife called up to him to say that *Sports Illustrated* was on the phone. He got so excited, he nicked himself shaving. He was so enthused about getting such national recognition that, as he rushed to the phone, he fell down the stairs and bruised himself. He got up and breathlessly grabbed the phone and said, "Hello." The voice on the other end said, "Yes, sir, I am happy to tell you that for only 75 cents per week, you can receive a one year's subscription . . . ."

There are times when we get ourselves all pumped up about something, only to be disappointed later. Drawing nearer to God will never disappoint. But, as we noticed in the previous chapter, before we can draw nearer to God, we have to draw away from some other things.

In 2 Timothy 2:15 there is a very good 3-point sermon. He begins with the word "study" in the KJV. The word actually means "give it your best shot." He goes on to say what he wants us to do. First, he says we should give it our best shot to be approved by God. Second, we should do our best to be a workman which has no reason to be ashamed. Last, we should give our best effort to handle God's word correctly. Being "approved by God" carries with it the idea of drawing nearer to Him. Paul expands that idea in verses 20-21 by introducing the concept of our trying to be "a vessel that is suited for use by the Lord." A vessel is simply an empty container which is worthless in and of itself. The value is in the contents of the vessel.

Paul tells us what contents we are supposed to hold in Philippians 1:20-21. He says, "Christ will be exalted in my body . . . For to me, to live is Christ and to die is gain." In other words, as vessels of God, we are filled up with Jesus' purposes for our lives. Galatians

2:20 says we are dead, and the lives we live are according to the Son of God's wishes. Our purposes are His purposes. Our choices are His choices. That is what it means to be a vessel which is "suited for use by the Lord." In doing these things, we will draw closer to God than we have ever been before.

As we go back to 2 Timothy 2, we find that, before this wonderful process begins, there are certain values we need to insert into our perspective on how we live. As we draw nearer to God by being vessels in His hands, we must learn to envision ourselves as workmen who need not be ashamed while handling God's word correctly.

Workmen Who Need Not Be Ashamed

Verse 15 says we should strive to be "a workman who does not need to be ashamed." Now, what prevents a workman from being ashamed? It is actually very simple. A workman has to do what is expected of him in order not to be ashamed. In Matthew 24:45-51 Jesus talks about two different kinds of servants. One He calls a "faithful and wise servant." This is the one who is doing what he is supposed to be doing the day his boss comes back home. Jesus refers to the other guy as a "wicked servant." He is the one who is in a drunken rage against his fellowservants when his boss comes home. So, it is clear that the workman who does not need to be ashamed is the one who does his job the way it is supposed to be done.

Paul does not leave us in the dark as to what God expects. In verse 22 he tells us to "flee the evil desires of youth." In 1 Thessalonians 4 he tells us why we should do this. He says, "God did not call us to be impure, but to live a holy life." In other words, God has no intention of His people being caught up in sin. The purpose of calling was to take us out of the sin of the world, and to have for Himself a pure and holy bride (Ephesians 5:25- 27). When we forsake that purpose, we are in a position of being ashamed before God. But, verse 22 goes on to mention some positive things we can do in our service to God. Righteousness, faith, love and peace are all things which we should be cultivating. The phrase "with those who call on the Lord out of a pure heart" shows that these are pri-

orities for everyone who really wants to please God. As these qualities are generated within us, we become workmen who have no
need of being ashamed.

There are times when Christians get confused about all of this.
It is extremely easy to be drawn into Satan's web of deceit and to
begin to do the very opposite of what God is telling us to do. There
was once a Navy pilot who was engaged in maneuvers. The admiral
in charge had ordered absolute radio silence. However, this young
pilot accidentally turned his radio on and was heard to say, "Boy,
am I confused!" The admiral grabbed the microphone and ordered
all channels to be opened immediately. He screamed into the microphone, "Will the pilot who broke radio silence identify himself
immediately!" After a prolonged silence, a soft voice came over the
radio, "I'm confused, but not that confused."

We cannot allow ourselves to be confused about our walk with
God. As we draw nearer to Him, we must draw away from anything
which would make us ashamed.

Handling God's Word Correctly

In verse 15, Paul tells us to "correctly handle the word of
truth." There is much confusion about what this means. In
1 Corinthians 2, Paul says the words he was speaking were the very
"wisdom of God." So, part of handling God's word correctly is
speaking God's wisdom and not your own. This is a very important
aspect of properly handling God's word, but it is *not* the only one.
There are some brethren who actually count the number of Bible
references in a sermon in order to judge whether it is "scriptural"
or not. As I have said, it is important to speak God's wisdom and
not your own, but filling a sermon up with Scripture does not mean
you are "correctly handling" God's word.

You do not have to leave 2 Timothy 2 to find out what the
phrase "correctly handling" really means in reference to God's
word. First, he tells us to avoid the wrong spirit in the way we use
God's word. In verses 23-24, he identifies the wrong spirit as being
an argumentative or quarrelsome one. This kind of spirit is wrong
no matter what the issue is. No issue in the world justifies the
absolute glee that some brethren get out of "a good argument."

79

Well, let's talk about issues for a moment. In verse 14 Paul says we should not argue about "words." That is a reference to questions and issues which are of no consequence whatever, usually arguments which are a matter of semantics. Paul says that arguing and debating about these things "only ruins those who listen." In other words, no one's spiritual growth is stimulated by those kinds of discussions.

Someone might say, "That is right! We should not be arguing about unimportant things. But the Bible tells us to 'earnestly contend for the faith.' That means it is OK to argue about the really important doctrinal issues." Let's see if that reasoning holds water. In verses 16-18, Paul says we must avoid "godless chatter." At first glance, it appears Paul is still talking about the unimportant matters of verse 14. However, if you keep on reading, you see that Paul is talking about something entirely different. He mentions the teachings of Hymenaeus and Philetus as an example of "godless chatter." What were these men teaching? They were teaching that the resurrection had already occurred and that there would be no resurrection in the future. The effect of their teaching is seen in the statement, "they destroy the faith of some."

This is clearly a very vital doctrinal matter. This is not a simple debate about "words." This is a matter of spiritual life and death for some. Yet, what does Paul say? He says, indulging in this kind of "godless chatter" causes the participants to become more and more ungodly. You do not have to listen to too many "contending for the faith" discussions between brethren to see the truth of that. Even in a single conversation, pride and arrogance begin oozing from the pores of the participants.

Paul also tells us that participating in these discussions actually has the effect of spreading the false teaching "like gangrene." There are times when a brother may be studying an issue and coming to some preliminary conclusions. When someone takes him to task over it, it has the effect of solidifying him in that position when he may have studied himself out of it if given the chance. There are other times when a brother is firmly entrenched in a false teaching, but it is confined to his region of the world. When well-meaning brothers jump on him through lectureships and magazines, it gives his false teaching national exposure and the problem becomes even worse. I have attended lectureships in which this very thing has happened. As I sat in the audience, the speaker began talking about a brother I had never heard of, from a town I was completely unfamiliar with, who was teaching something that was clearly wrong. Now, what sense does it make to do this? If the brother was left alone or if the preacher had handled it privately with the brother, the false teaching he was doing would likely have never left his home town. But when we give false teaching national exposure, it spreads like wildfire, and many people get hurt by it.

So how do we handle false teaching if we cannot argue or quarrel about it? Well, we can try a novel approach — we can teach the truth. You see, if I clearly set out the truth of God's word, everyone who listens will be able to identify false teaching when they hear it. This is "correctly handling" God's word in a manner which does not cause false teaching to spread. But, Paul goes on to identify the "right spirit" in opposing false teaching and handling God's word correctly. Verses 24-26 say that, rather than being quarrelsome, we should teach others with gentleness, patience and meekness. We see this spirit in Jesus as He was talking to the Samaritan woman at Jacob's Well. She did her best to start a religious argument with Him, but Jesus did not bite. Instead, he gently led that woman through the conversation until she was convinced He was the Messiah of God. At no time in the discussion did Jesus accuse or berate the woman in any way.

At this point, critics would say, "Yes, but Jesus did not treat the Pharisees gently. He really told them how the cow ate the cabbage." That is very true, but the Pharisees were not honest seekers of truth. They were hypocritical men with hidden agendas which did not include pleasing the Father. We are not talking about those kind of people. We are talking about people who believe some false teaching, but are sincere and honest in their search for truth. You never find Jesus being critical of those kind of people.

Verses 25-26 identify our goal as we instruct someone in error. If we are "correctly handling" God's word, our goal for teaching people in error is for God to "grant them repentance leading them to a knowledge of the truth," and for them to "come to their senses and escape from the trap of the devil." At no point in our discussion should my goal be to win the argument. There is no justification for publicizing the disagreement in order to show the brotherhood how "sound" I am and to be invited on the lectureship circuit. My goal must never be to humiliate my brother nor to slander his reputation by applying ungodly labels to him. God's goal for me in these discussions is simple and clear — to help my brother draw closer to his Father. When that motive becomes mixed with any other motive, I am not "correctly handling" God's word, regardless of how many Scriptures I use in my sermon!!! Drawing nearer to God demands that we avoid handling God's word incorrectly!

The journey of spiritual growth and communion with God is a long and rocky one. The closer you get in your walk with God, the further you realize you have to go. Still, it is not a futile effort. On the contrary, it is a joyful and delightful journey! But as we attempt to draw nearer to God, we must turn away from anything which would make us ashamed before Him. We also have to stay away from attitudes which cause us to mishandle God's holy word.

It is time for us to realize our need to draw closer to God. It is also important for us to realize we do not have forever to do it! You know, God has given each one of us a heart. The work it does is vital to our lives, but we take it for granted because it beats all by itself without any effort from us. When we exercise, it speeds up. When we rest, it slows down. But one day, and none of us knows just when it will happen, our heart is going to STOP! When that happens, will you be found drawing nearer to God or will you be following after something else?

Discussion Questions

1. Why does God want us to "give our best shot" to what we do for Him?

2. As vessels of God, what should be our contents?

3. What specific things can we do to avoid being ashamed before God?

4. In what ways can we handle God's word incorrectly?

5. Why do some insist on arguing about false teaching in spite of God's warnings in this regard?

6. If we cannot argue and quarrel about false teaching, what should we be doing to assure it does not get a foothold among us?

7. Why is it so difficult to maintain the proper spirit when we disagreee about doctrinal matters? What attitudes must we be careful to avoid?

Chapter 11
Maintaining My Focus

People have a variety of reasons for attending worship services. Sometimes they have an honest desire to send praises up to God. At other times, people are drawn to worship by gimmickry. I read about one church which had a performing horse at the church building. The people came to see how smart this horse was. The trainer asked the horse how many commandments there are, and the horse stomped 10 times. The trainer asked the horse how many apostles there are, and the horse stomped 12 times. A skeptic in the crowd asked the horse how many hypocrites there are in the church, and the horse went into a dance on all fours.

Many have shallow reasons for attending worship. David had a different perspective in Psalm 100. He begins that psalm by saying, "Make a joyful noise to the Lord . . . ." He is clearly talking about offering worship up to God in that verse. He uses phrases like "come before His presence with singing," "we are His people," "we are the sheep of His pasture," "enter into His gates with thanksgiving," and a number of others. Each of these statements shows that as we worship God, we are drawing nearer to Him. In fact, drawing nearer to God is the very heart of what worship is all about. We do not limit any of this discussion to the public worship assembly. Actually, very little is said in Scripture regarding the public worship assembly. Almost everything that is said applies to worship in general, whether it is public or private.

In John 4, Jesus is responding to the challenge of the Samaritan woman who suggested that the Jews were wrong for saying that Jerusalem was the place people ought to worship. Rather than getting into a religious discussion with her, Jesus simply said "a time is coming and has now come when the true worshipers will worship the Father in spirit and truth, for they are the kind of worshipers the Father seeks" (verse 23). Note the longing in the heart of God for us to worship Him. The reason for this immense longing is because God desperately wants us to draw closer to Him. Jesus says the hour will come when people who truly love God will worship Him in a way that will draw them closer to Him. The hour Jesus predicted has arrived! It is time, right now, for true worshipers of God to draw near to Him in praise and adoration both in private communion and in public worship.

Many sermons have been preached relative to the outward mechanics of worship and how God has directed us to worship Him. This is *not* the focus of this chapter. Our emphasis is on those inward things which give those outward mechanics meaning. In order for our worship to draw us nearer to God, it must be correct, consistent and contrite.

Correct

This is the point at which many people go into a lengthy dissertation about the outward mechanics which God demands in our public worship. This approach misses the point for two reasons. First, there is little if any specific reference to a public worship assembly in the New Testament. Second, there is no specific direction as to how we are supposed to conduct our public worship assemblies. However, when it comes to worshiping correctly, there is an abundance of instruction regarding what should be happening *on the inside*. First, in order for our worship to be correct, it must come from a *forgiving* heart. In Matthew 5 Jesus refers to a situation in which a person "offers his gift at the altar." Obviously, bringing your gift to the altar is an act of worship. Jesus says, if we enter into a worship situation and we remember that someone is upset with us about something, we must "leave our gift there in front of the altar." Leaving our gift at the altar means we stop our worship. Can you imagine Jesus telling us not to worship God? What circumstances could possibly arise which would make worship inappropriate? Jesus says we should go make things right with our brother, and then "offer our gift." In other words, if our relationship with others is not right, then our worship is not right either! Sometimes this means we need to forgive someone. At other times it requires us to ask for their forgiveness. Whichever case it may be, worshiping correctly demands that we make things right with our brothers.

Second, in order for our worship to be correct, it must come from a *reflecting* heart. In 1 Corinthians 11 Paul talks about the importance of observing the Lord's Supper with the proper attitude. The only attitude to have while observing this sacred time is an attitude of reflecting back on what Jesus did for you on the cross, and how He was raised again the third day. Later in this context Paul refers to this attitude as, "discerning the Lord's body." That is where God wants our minds to be as we take the Lord's Supper. He does not want us thinking about the football game that is coming on, or the roast that may be burning in the oven. He does not want us concentrating on the tempo of the singing or on the temperature of the room. God wants our complete focus to be on the sacrifice of His dear Son! If we allow our minds to wander aimlessly to other things, we are not worshiping correctly. Consequently, we are not drawing any nearer to God.

Finally, in order for our worship to be correct, it must come from a *sincere* heart. In Mark 15:19, it says that the Roman soldiers bowed down and "worshiped" Jesus. In verse 20 it says, "after they had mocked Him . . . ." Now wait a minute. Verse 19 says they worshiped, and verse 20 says they mocked. Which was it? Well, both are accurate statements. They were worshiping in what they were saying, but it was a mockery because they did not mean a word of it. You see, that is precisely what makes our worship a mockery. It is not enough to sing words of praise to God; we must mean them. It is not sufficient to pray words of adoration to our Father. The words must come from the depths of our heart. If we are insincere in what we say, then we are mocking Jesus just like the Roman soldiers did.

For some reason, we think that a lie ceases to be a lie when we set it to music. When the church sings, "All To Jesus I Surrender," and half the people in the church have not surrendered anything to Jesus, it is a lie. When the congregation rings out the chorus of "This World Is Not My Home," and many of the people feel very much at home in this world, it is a lie. If it is a lie, it is a mockery.

In order for us to draw nearer to God in our worship, we must be correct on the inside by having a forgiving, reflecting and sincere heart.

Consistent

When we say our worship must be consistent, we are not talking about the frequency of our worship (although that is important too). When we talk about consistency, we are talking about our worship in comparison to our life. In order for our worship to truly draw us nearer to God, it must have some resemblance to how we live. Too often, the worship we offer up to God comes from lives which are not consistent with that worship. I recently heard about a man who was reading his newspaper at the breakfast table while his wife was cooking at the stove. He said to his wife, "Hey, listen to this. The cashier at the bank has absconded with $100,000. Not only that, but he stole one of the bank executive's limousines, and ran off with the bank president's wife." "My, that is awful," exclaimed the wife, "I wonder who they will get to teach his Sunday School class next week?" Stories like that would be funny if they were not so true.

God demands that our worship be consistent with our lives. This does not mean we have to be perfect before we can worship God. Many people believe that, and they will not attend a worship service. That is an inappropriate extreme. However, living your life without regard to God's will during the week and then offering up worship to Him as a salve for your conscience is equally wrong.

Isn't that what the Pharisees were doing? Jesus told the people of His day that their righteousness had to exceed the righteousness of the Pharisees if they wanted to please God (Matthew 5:20). Throughout the remainder of that passage, Jesus identifies inward qualities of character which God's people must acquire. The Pharisees had the outward motions of keeping the law down to an art. But the inward qualities of character which God wanted them to have totally eluded them. Because of this, they had a righteousness problem. They were not drawing nearer to God in their walk with Him. In Matthew 23:4 Jesus says they bound heavy burdens on other people that they were not willing to bear themselves. In other words, they were hypocritical, power-hungry people who were more interested in keeping their authority positions than they were in drawing closer to God. Their talk did not match their walk. Their profession did not match their performance. Their piety did not fit with their practices. As a result, their worship was not consistent with their lives. Jesus described them as people who honored God with their lips and drew near to God with their mouths, but their hearts were one hundred miles away (Matthew 15:8). That is no way for us to live if we want to draw near to God!

Contrite

Where has reverence been hiding these days? Where is the constant awareness of the magnificence of God today? Reverence has been replaced by routine. Noticing God's magnificence has been replaced by noticing the temperature of the building, noticing the time on the clock and noticing the clothes people are wearing.

In order for our worship to draw us near to God, we must be impressed anew with His presence. Read Exodus 19:16-18 as well as Exodus 20:18-19. These verses give an extremely impressive description of what it was like when God appeared in the presence of His people. The mountain was full of smoke and lightning, the ground trembled, and Moses was so frightened by the scene that he said, "I am trembling with fear" (Hebrews 12:21).

We see a similar scene in Isaiah 6 where God appears to Isaiah in a vision. The glory of God filled the temple. Isaiah saw the bigness of God, and his own unworthiness. That is always the reaction of people who have truly been in the presence of God. When John saw the glorified person of Jesus, he fell down at the feet of the Saviour and appeared to be dead (Revelation 1:17). It is indisputable from these passages that God's presence made a difference to these people. It made them see their own weakness and God's strength. It caused them to realize their own inadequacies and God's amazing ability. It forced them to understand their own dirtiness and God's holiness. I wonder how these people behaved as they were standing in the very presence of God. Do you think it was similar to our assemblies today? Do you think they were passing notes to one another? Do you think they were telling jokes and giggling? Do you think they were leaving to go to the bathroom or to be the first one in line at the cafeteria? Do you think they were watching the clock and wondering when this was going to be over? You say you doubt that any of these things took place?

So do I. If we want our worship to draw us nearer to God, they will not take place among us either!

At times we take the privilege of worship for granted. Many feel it is their gift to God, and they assume that anything they offer is acceptable to Him. Strike one! They think that any type of worship will please God. Strike two!! Many feel the act of worship automatically draws us closer to God. Strike three!!! Worship can draw us much closer to God, but it must be correct, consistent and contrite. If any one of these characteristics is missing, our worship will actually result in driving us further from God.

The following article was written by my brother, David Tappe. It accurately depicts what happens in the hearts of many Christians during any given worship assembly.

It was a typical Sunday morning. Hey, only 10 minutes late for class. That's a new record. Now I wish I had not come – they are talking about giving. Man, it was easy for me to look around that class and see who it was that had been cheating God!

Once class was over, on the way to the assembly, my mind focused on the pressing issue of the day – When at the cafeteria, will I have the fish or the chicken? I knew it was going to be a bad day when I went into the auditorium and saw some stranger sitting in my seat. Can't we find someone else to lead singing? Every time this guy does, we sing songs I don't know. I don't guess it matters that much since I don't sing anyway. I see **he** is scheduled to lead the opening prayer. You can count on the service running over. Here comes the plate. I think I'll double my giving today. Let's see now, where did I put that other dollar? Oh, not another sermon on evangelism! Does that guy think that's the only function of the church?

Finally, the invitation song! Now, if no one responds, I will have a good start to the cafeteria. It never fails, the elders have a special announcement. Now, if people just won't hold me up, I can get a pretty good place in line. I'll just use the old "side door pretend not to hear anyone" exit. It works every time.

Man, two full hours of church and I show up even though I don't get anything out of it. I sure hope God was taking note. I've made a decision – it will be the chicken."

You know, God *is* taking notes in our worship assemblies. But he is not noticing who is there and who is not there. Rather, God is making note of who is drawing closer to Him in their worship and who is just playing games!

Discussion Questions

1. What are some shallow reasons for attending worship services?

2. What relationship is there between worship and drawing nearer to God?

3. What is necessary before our worship can draw us nearer to God?

4. In your own words, what ways must our worship be inwardly correct?

5. What does it mean to say that our worship must be consistent? Give some examples.

6. What is the difference between being "consistent" and being "perfect?"

7. In what ways should we be contrite in our worship?

8. Why is contrition such a difficult attitude to maintain throughout our worship?

9. When you really stand in the presence of God, what effects will it have on you and your attitude? How can we maintain these attitudes throughout our lives?

Chapter 12
Guarding Against Dehydration

We noticed in the previous chapter that drawing nearer to God is something which can get us very excited. However, as great as enthusiasm is, it is not worth very much by itself. It reminds me of the small factory which had to stop operations because an essential machine broke down. No one could get it to work. Finally, in an act of desperation, they called an outside expert to come in. The man looked over the situation, took a hammer, and gently tapped the machine in a certain spot. The machine immediately turned on and started working perfectly. When the expert submitted his bill for $100, the owner of the plant hit the roof. He demanded an itemized bill. The expert submitted the bill as follows: "For hitting the machine — $1.00; For knowing where to hit — $99.00." You see, it is not enough just to hit something. You have to know where to hit it. Our enthusiasm about spiritual things and drawing nearer to God is great. But, we really need to know "where to hit it." In other words, we must develop a knowledge of how the process works.

This is where Bible study comes in. But studying the Bible is different from any other kind of study in one important respect. Hebrews 4:12 says the word of God is "living and active." There was an episode on "Star Trek: The Next Generation" where a guy had an incurable disease in addition to being very old. In order to solve his problem, he injected some kind of living organism inside his body which worked to cure his disease and to make him younger. By the end of the episode, the guy was completely healthy and in his early thirties.

This makes for a very interesting science fiction story, but it clearly has no relationship to reality — or does it? There may be no physical way for this to happen, but when you look at the living word of God, the process that takes place within the human heart is very similar. When a Christian studies the Bible for the purpose of drawing closer to God, he actually injects within his heart a living, active organism.

When the word enters our hearts and we allow it to rule there, it will transform our lives.

The Word Entering the Heart

James encourages us to "accept the word planted" into our hearts (James 1:21). This happens when a person first becomes a Christian. Romans 10 spells out this process in much finer detail. Paul says, "everyone who calls on the name of the Lord will be saved" (verse 13). Then, he goes into a series of questions which show how this comes about in people's lives. He asks, "How, then, can they call on the one they have not believed in? And how can they believe in the one of whom they have not heard. And how can they hear without someone preaching to them?" (verses 14-15a). The conclusion of all of these questions is that faith comes through hearing God's word.

In Acts 2, Peter preached a powerful sermon about the identity of Jesus from Old Testament prophecy. When the people heard God's word preached, they were "cut to the heart." As Lydia was listening to the preaching of Paul, "the Lord opened her heart to respond to Paul's message." Certainly, God's word has a powerful effect once it enters the human heart. That is why it is called "the power of God for the salvation of everyone who believes" (Romans 1:16). Each of these are powerful illustrations of God's mighty word entering human hearts and having a tremendous impact. The extent of that impact is the next thing we need to consider.

The Word Ruling the Heart

Once the living word of God has been injected into our hearts, it begins to do its work. The first thing that happens when God's word enters the heart of a person is that his will begins changing. Philippians 2:13 says God works inside us "both to will and to act according to his good purpose." Most of the time we only look at the "act" side of God's will. We all know that, when we allow God to work in us, we will do many of the outward acts of obedience that He desires of us. But, before we ever get to the "act" side of His desire for us, we come to the "will" side. In this verse, Paul tells us God not only helps us to *do* His good pleasure, but he also helps us to *want to do* His good pleasure.

So, the heart is where God's transforming power in our lives really begins! Romans 12 talks about being transformed and fashioned by the renewing of our minds. Ephesians 2 mentions being renewed in the spirit of our minds. Regardless of how you phrase it, God's word begins ruling our hearts when it starts transforming our will. That is very important when you realize the strength of the human will. Many great and amazing things have been accomplished in this world by someone's tenacious will to get it done. Every day decisions are made in our lives according to what we want to do. So, if you are going to rule the heart and the life of someone, you had better get in the driver's seat of his will. That is where God starts.

Once the transformation has begun in our wills, God's word alters our perspective. Colossians 3:15 encourages us to allow the peace of Jesus to "rule in our hearts." In verse 16 he says, "let the word of Christ dwell in you richly." It is impossible to separate the word of Jesus in our heart from the peace we have in Him. When we are filled with the peace of Jesus, our entire way of thinking begins to change.

The world has its own set of priorities and agendas. Most of us buy into these things as we grow up in this world. From this perspective, the world's ways seem to make a great deal of sense, and God's ways appear to be rather silly. As God's word begins to rule our hearts, this whole way of thinking reverses. We slowly come to see that the ways of the world are extremely short-sighted, and God's ways make more and more sense everyday. Once this perspective begins to set in, we realize that God's ways are best for us!

When God's word rules our hearts, it becomes very apparent that we are drawing nearer to Him. In the Old Testament, God looked into the future and saw His people in the New Testament age (including us). He gives a detailed description of the kind of relationship we would have with Him under the New Covenant. This Old Testament prediction (Jeremiah 31:31-34) is recalled in Hebrews 8:10 where it says, "This is the covenant I will make with the house of Israel after that time . . . I will put my laws in their minds and write them on their hearts. I will be their God, and they will be my people." When He says, "I will write my laws on their hearts," He is referring to the process we have described. In the Old Testament era, God's laws were written down. Anytime His people wanted to know God's will, they had to pick it up and read it. Today, the will of God is indelibly inscribed on the hearts of every person who really wants to please Him. What is the result of the word of God being written in our hearts? He says He would be a God to us and we would be His people. From the early days of the Old Testament, God's intent was that we draw near to Him in an intimate communion relationship. This is only possible as we allow God's word to enter our hearts and to begin ruling there!

The Word Transforming the Life

When God's word enters and begins to rule our hearts, it is only a matter of time before our lives start changing radically. We already noticed Colossians 3:16 which instructs us to allow God's word to fill us up. The very next verse says, "Whatever you do, whether in word or deed, do it all in the name of the Lord Jesus." When a person is filled up with God's word and the changes begin to happen in his heart, he will turn complete control of his life over to the will of Jesus. Whether it is something he says or does, that person is going to be willing to give it all to Christ. He knows that just hearing God's word does not get the job done. He realizes that genuine nearness to God can only be consummated when he becomes a doer of God's word (James 1:22).

What happens when you inject a living organism into your blood stream? That is a question that should be reserved for science fiction writers to answer. But there is nothing "science fiction" about the impact of injecting the spiritually living organism of God's word into our hearts. First, it enters our heart when we really accept it. Then, it works on our hearts until it has filled us up and begun ruling. When that occurs, radical changes begin taking place in the way we live our lives. At each of these stages of transformation, we find we are drawing nearer and nearer to God.

Before any of this can happen, we have to open our Bibles and read. None of this happens by osmosis, and it certainly does not occur accidentally. There was once a young woman who read a certain book and put it on her shelf, thinking it was the dullest book she had ever read. Later, she met a young man of whom she began to grow quite fond. In fact, their friendship blossomed into love, and it was not long until they were engaged to be married. One evening, she happened to recall the book she had read. It was written by a man who had the same name as her fiance. When she mentioned it to him, he told her that he had written that book. This amazed the woman so much that she decided to read the book again. She sat up until early one morning reading and found it to be the most interesting book she had ever read. Why did her opinion of the book change so much? She had fallen in love with its author! You know, the same thing will happen to you in your Bible study. You may have studied your Bible in the past, and you may have found it to be rather dull and difficult to understand. But once you fall deeply in love with the Author, the Bible will come alive to you and you will never be the same again!

Discussion Questions

1. What are some good things about having enthusiasm?

2. What are some weaknesses if enthusiasm is all you have?

3. What are the differences between a "living, active word" and a regular book?

4. How does God's word initially enter our hearts?

5. Once in our hearts, what effect does it begin to have on us?

6. When the word begins to rule our hearts, what specific things begin to change?

7. How is this related to our drawing closer to God?

8. What is the natural result of the word entering and ruling our heart?

Chapter 13
Finding the Source of Staying Power

You know, when a person does not know the Bible very well, he misuses it and forces it to say what he already believes. This happened after a hotly contested basketball game once. The referee was walking off the floor when a fellow came up to him and gave him a piece of paper. On the paper, the guy had written two Scripture references — Matthew 27:5 and Luke 10:37. When the referee got home, he pulled out his Bible and looked up the verses. Matthew 27:5 says, "And Judas . . . went out and hanged himself." Luke 10:37 says, "Go and do thou likewise." The referee got the message!

The same thing happens regarding the Holy Spirit. Many do not know much about Him. As a result, many abuse Him by saying He does things which He never promised to do. Others respond to that by neglecting the subject of the Holy Spirit entirely. This is an extremely unfortunate knee-jerk reaction. Romans 8 shows what a special gift the Holy Spirit is to God's children. We must be careful not to misuse that gift. We must also be very careful not to neglect it. The only way to avoid these two extremes is to understand what God says about the Holy Spirit and His role in helping us to draw nearer to our Father.

Romans 8:11 teaches that the Holy Spirit actually lives in the hearts of God's children. Just like the living word has its impact on our lives, so does the Spirit of God as He dwells within us. In order to draw us nearer to God, the Holy Spirit changes our minds, which changes our lives, and all the while He is interceding for us with the Father.

Changes Our Minds

Romans 8:5-8 points out the contrast between the mindset of the world and the mindset of the Spirit. These two viewpoints are so contradictory that you cannot hold to both of them at the same time. They are also very different in their results. The mindset of the world causes us to die spiritually. In addition, if you hold to the world's mindset, it is impossible to please God (verse 8). On the other hand, the mindset of the Spirit helps us to focus on the things which the Spirit wants for us. The result of that is life and peace.

As we mentioned in a previous chapter, the mindset of the world is divided into two categories. First, there is the clearly sinful mindset. Ephesians 2:3 talks about the days when we were controlled by this way of thinking. In that verse, Paul says, "All of us lived among them at one time, gratifying the cravings of our sinful nature and following its desires and thoughts." There is no way we can draw closer to God as long as we are following the orders of our sinful nature. The sin we pursue acts like a giant wall between us and God. The only way to break through that wall and get to God is to allow His Spirit to change our way of thinking.

The second aspect of the world's mindset is the subtle, common sense mindset. We have discussed this in detail earlier, so we only briefly mention it here. The world says we should love those who love us back. The world says we should take care of ourselves and our families first. The world teaches us to enter into the "rat race" in a struggle to get the most power and prestige possible. The world emphasizes the here and now of the present: "Eat, drink and be merry, for tomorrow we die."

God's Spirit enters our lives and He changes both of these ways of thinking. Instead of satisfying our sinful desires, He teaches us to satisfy God's spiritual desires for us. If the Holy Spirit is working inside us, we will not work to satisfy the desires of our flesh (Galileans 5:16). If we have God's Spirit and we are genuinely trying to draw closer to Him, we will be dead to the passions of our former nature (Galatians 5:24). Clearly, we are not talking about perfection here. We are not saying that people who are developing a spiritual mindset do not ever sin again. We are simply talking about the dominant influence in our life. Those who are striving for the mindset of the Spirit follow after those things which help them to overcome the world's sinful mindset (1 Timothy 6:11-12).

The Spirit also helps us to replace the world's logic with God's wisdom. The world tells us to stop loving when the love is not returned. God's Spirit helps us to love those who hate us. The world says to "look out for #1." God's Spirit says to put others before ourselves. The world says to take revenge. The Spirit of God says to give forgiveness. The world says to seek wealth. The Spirit says to seek Heaven. The Spirit totally alters our outlook on life. That is why Paul tells us to set our minds on heavenly things and not on earthly things (Colossians 3:1).

As God's Spirit moves within us to change our minds, we find ourselves drawing nearer to our Father.

Changes Our Lives

Going back to Romans 8, we find the mindset we maintain determines the lifestyle we pursue (verses 12-17). So, when a person turns his back on a worldly mindset and pursues a Spirit-centered mindset, his lifestyle will experience a corresponding change. This is commonly called "conversion." There is a lot of confusion about what conversion really is. A certain preacher discovered this when he was questioning a Sunday School class concerning the definitions of many different religious terms. The class was doing fairly well until he asked, "What is conversion?" A young boy in the class thought for a moment and then answered, "It is the extra point after a touchdown!" That is the extent of understanding that many have of conversion. And yet, true spiritual conversion is so much more.

A truly converted person, once he has stopped living like a child of the devil, will begin living like a child of God (Romans 8:14-17). This means we have to live pure and holy lives (I John 3:2-3). It means that, not only must our "walk" match *our "talk,"* but it must also match *Jesus' "walk."* That is when we genuinely begin to seek God's kingdom before anything else. That is when we seek the needs of others above our own. That is when we see the wisdom in trading wealth and status for a right relationship with God. God's Spirit works in us to effect all of these changes.

Paul tells us what it means to live like a child of the devil. He tells us what it means to live like a child of God. The only remaining question is, which describes your life most often? Each of us could fall into either of these categories at any given time of our lives, but which fits you most often? Your answer to that question will reveal how much influence you are allowing God's Spirit to have in your heart.

Intercedes for Us

Up to this point, it sounds like the Spirit does the same things for us the word does (See the previous chapter). Since the Spirit makes use of the word to do many things, there are many similarities. However, there are many distinct differences between the word and the Spirit. For instance, the Spirit of God intercedes for us when we pray (Romans 8:26-27). There are times when we simply do not know what to say to God. At those times, the Spirit takes over and communicates to God for us with words which we could never express for ourselves. But prayer is only one of the ways in which He intercedes for us.

The Spirit assists us in our spiritual growth by helping us to develop qualities of character which we could never attain on our own. Since it is a growing process, we fail at times. As we grow in our walk with Jesus, we will fall occasionally. When we do, the Spirit is there to lift us to our feet, dust us off, and put us back on our way again. We find that each time we get up from falling down, we are a little further down the road than we were before we fell, and our journey continues. What a special thing it is to have the Spirit interceding for us in our lives!

In addition to these things, God's Spirit bears witness along with our Spirit that we are children of God (Romans 8:16). That sounds strange to us, but the Jews were very aware of the significance of this. Under the old law, a person could be convicted of a crime and put to death if there were 2 or 3 witnesses against him. So, having witnesses in a court situation had a great deal of meaning. On the day of judgment, when we all stand before God, everyone will know whether they are saved or lost. Before the final verdict is handed down, many will be claiming to be children of God (Matthew 7:21-23). It is kind of like those sports fans who wait until the end of a season before they really support a team. When it is obvious who is going to win, they start supporting that team as though they had been a faithful fan from the start of the season. What a joke it is to have this kind of fickle commitment. But when we all stand before God, no one will be laughing at that joke. You can claim to be a child of God all you want. You can dig into your memory and come up with many good and noble deeds which you did while you were alive. You can offer up the times you went to church as evidence of your Christian identity. But, none of this will do you any good. Why? Because you do not have a second witness to stand beside you. That is where the Holy Spirit comes in.

Jerry Clower tells the story of a woman who lived in Amite County, Mississippi. She lived near a construction site and the workers were tarring the roof of a nearby house. The lady had 16 children, and one of them came up missing one day. She looked for him everywhere, and finally discovered that he had slipped into a 50 gallon drum of black roofing tar. She reached down, pulled him up, took a look at him, and shoved him back into the drum of tar. She said, "Boy, it would be easier to have another one than to clean you up!" You know, that must be just how God feels when He looks at my life! I mess up so badly at times! But He never gives up on me. He always lifts me out of the drum, washes me off and patiently sends me on my way again.

In this section, we have talked about drawing nearer to God. God has made substantial efforts to help us draw closer to Him. But you know, God issues invitations – not draft notices. If you are waiting for God to impose His will on you so that you have no choice but to draw closer to Him, you will be waiting a long time. God is not going to force you. But God will run the length of the road to meet you if He sees you take the first step toward Him! Praise His holy Name!!!

Discussion Questions

1. In what ways have some misused the subject of the Holy Spirit?

2. In what ways have some neglected the study of the Holy Spirit?

3. Why do humans tend toward the extremes in this area?

4. Why is God's Spirit such a special gift to us?

5. In what ways does God's Spirit change our minds?

6. What are some aspects of the world's logic that God's Spirit wants to change in our minds?

7. What is involved in genuine conversion?

8. Why do some people have such a superficial understanding of conversion?

9. In what specific ways does the Spirit intercede for us?

About the Author

Craig Tappe has been the pulpit minister at Alvarado Church of Christ in Alvarado, Texas since 1987. For Craig's first five years in ministry he served as youth and education minister. He graduated from LeTourneau University with a B.S. in Business Management and has attended Oklahoma Christian College. He has written numerous books and study guides. Craig has also written numerous articles for *The Christian Bible Teacher*. Craig has served on the Alvarado City Council and as Mayor. He and his wife, Melodie, have three children: Tiffany, Kristen and Brandon. His hobbies include writing and tennis.